William & Rosalie

A HOLOCAUST TESTIMONY

by
William and Rosalie Schiff
and Craig Hanley

Number 1 in the Mayborn Literary Nonfiction Series

University of North Texas Press
Mayborn Graduate Institute of Journalism
Denton, Texas

10 9 8 7 6 5 4 3

Permissions:
University of North Texas Press
1155 Union Circle #311336
Denton, TX 76203-5017

The paper used in this book meets the minimum requirements of the American National Standard for Permanence of Paper for Printed Library Materials, z39.48.1984. Binding materials have been chosen for durability.

Library of Congress Cataloging-in-Publication Data

Schiff, William 1918–
  William & Rosalie : a Holocaust testimony / by William and Rosalie Schiff and Craig Hanley. – 1st ed.
     p. cm. – (Mayborn literary nonfiction series ; no. 1)
  Includes bibliographical references.
  ISBN 978-1-57441-237-6 (cloth : alk. paper)
  ISBN 978-1-57441-261-1 (paper : alk. paper)
  1. Schiff, William 1918– 2. Jews–Poland–Krakow–Biography.
3. Holocaust, Jewish (1939–1945)–Poland–Personal narratives.
4. Holocaust survivors–Texas–Dallas–Biography. 5. Krakow (Poland)
–Biography. I. Schiff, Rosalie 1922– II. Hanley, Craig 1958–
III. Title. IV. Title: William and Rosalie.
  DS134.72.S35A3 2007
  940.53'18092243862–dc22
  [B]

                                                                    2007009530

William & Rosalie: A Holocaust Testimony is
Number 1 in the Mayborn Literary Nonfiction Series

Contents

Family photographs appear after chapter six.

PREFACE BY CRAIG HANLEY

In a roundabout way this book began a year before I met William and Rosalie Schiff. In the summer of 2004, I was watching the news on CSPAN. The main story involved Israel and viewers, as usual, were encouraged to phone in their thoughts. Fans of this particular program are accustomed to the occasional caller who cannot control his or her political passion, but the flood of hostility that morning was so steady and intense the host seemed shocked by the suddenly dark tone of his show.

There were denunciations of "the Jewish mafia" in the United States and claims that the Jewish state was responsible for 9/11 and for the death of American soldiers in Iraq. There was a demand for the White House to sever ties with its closest ally in the Middle East. Callers with a variety of regional accents were cautioned for their remarks and the more furious had to be disconnected.

It was a surprisingly ugly morning in America.

To get some background on the issues, I offered to volunteer a few days a week at the Houston Chapter of the American Jewish Committee. The executive director was tremendously hospitable and let me pitch in on minor chores. I watched the organization respond to the media firestorm created by Mel Gibson's *The Passion of the Christ* and review recent legislation designed to protect places of worship from terror attacks. It was news to me as a Christian that a long established American minority had to maintain these sorts of proactive public relations and defense strategies.

Out of the blue, a friend in Dallas called and said a client of hers was looking for someone to write a book about his parents. She said, "They're Holocaust survivors who teach people about the dangers of hate." The project sounded remarkably in line with my recent interests and I met with Michael Schiff, one of the driving forces behind the Dallas Holocaust Museum. Due in large part to the experiences of his family, Mike has a serious interest in mass hate as a social phenomenon.

He did not want this book to be a relentless tale of misery, and fortunately his parents have lived their lives in a way that offers a strong message of hope. They have also lived long enough to connect the Nazi genocide directly to our modern age of suicide bombers and burning towers. At eighty-eight and eighty-four, respectively, William and Rosalie Schiff are still waging a personal educational crusade that has deeply touched thousands of students and adults in North Texas.

During months of interviews, I got to know two people whose young lives in Poland were just as normal as ours before the current terror war began. Their biographies are parables we would be foolish to ignore, and their courageous response to the hardships they suffered is a lesson in how much good a single human being—or two—can accomplish in a relatively short period of time.

This is not a sentimental book, but many tears had to be shed and re-shed to make sure we got the facts straight. Day after day, the Schiffs went back sixty-five years in time to relive the loss of their families and their entrapment in the Krakow ghetto and subsequent journey through six different Nazi camps. While those events form the bulk of the narrative, in a real sense the story begins at the end, in the normal

American city where they continue their low-key and highly effective teaching.

I believe William is right when he describes this book as a love story. It contains plenty of the horrors that modern civilizations are capable of when, as Rosalie likes to say, "human beings take off their masks." But after all the torture, the moral belongs to the survivors. The Schiffs tell it quickly and unpretentiously, and offer some timely advice on how to deal with mass hate, an evil that plagues the world now more than ever.

The story is built around personal recollections in normalized English. Longer first-person passages, from William or Rosalie or others, are inset and set in a slightly different typeface.

chapter one

"When will people stop hating?"

On this lovely Thursday at the end of summer the citizens of Krakow move as usual through some of the finest architecture in Europe. Towering gothic churches, stately Renaissance homes and trendy cafes with gilt lettering crowd together around the main square. The true heart of the city is the storybook castle up on the hill where the Polish kings are buried. Below its thick wall flows the shimmering Vistula River.

It's 1939 and radio is a big deal. People are amazed the technology can bring them news from the other side of the earth. Inspired by the breakthrough, many students at the university are obsessed with math and electronics. Four centuries earlier Copernicus learned enough math here to figure out that the earth goes around the sun.

Not everybody is caught up in the radio craze, however. The bearded men in long black silk coats walking under the iron streetlamps spend a good bit of their time mastering ancient religious texts. Some believe in a miracle-worker who lived in the dark mountains on the horizon where melting snow feeds the river.

Horse hoofs echo through the cobbled streets as wagons bring food in from the countryside and supplies to stores and shops. Twelve of the wagons belong to Benzion Baum. He and his partners sell firewood to bakeries, candy makers, and hundreds of homes. Twenty-five years ago it was just Benzion in one wagon. He carried the split trunks through front doors and back doors, making neat stacks by stoves, bread ovens, and pots of bubbling chocolate.

Customers liked the wood vendor. He was dependable, earnest, and fair. Today he owns a yard on the other side of the river where twenty employees unload wood from train cars into the delivery wagons. In the new factory next door thirty more workers can't keep up with orders for the insulation product Benzion designed ten years ago. During harsh Polish winters it helps people save money on firewood.

Benzion lives at 7 Dietlovska Street, a prestigious address in a neighborhood called Kazimierz, home to most of the 70,000 Jews in the city. His wife's name is Helena and the couple have two girls and a boy. His oldest daughter, Rosalie, is sixteen.

> Our apartment was not far from downtown on a tree-lined street a few blocks from the river. From our windows we could see the Vistula and the castle on top of Wawel Hill. Mom and Dad gave us a home full of love. As committed as he was to his work, he stayed home if one of the kids was sick.
>
> My sister Lucy was fourteen and my little brother Henry was eight. We played in the parks and jumped on the backs of the wagons the horses pulled up and down our street. In winter we went sledding and on

sunny days we played kickball. In Poland back then
children didn't have many toys or dolls. In my favorite
game you tried to flick pebbles into a hole with your
finger. I kept coming home with dirty hands and Mom
was afraid I was turning into a tomboy.

I went to a little school not far from home. History was my favorite subject so I loved it when our
class went to the castle. It has an ancient hall with
a winding stair that goes way down into the dark.
This was supposed to be the cave of Smoke, the Krakow dragon. When we were little we were terrified of
Smoke because the legend says he liked to eat children.
None of us was afraid of the Germans because we
were not informed about politics at all. At that age I
never really thought about being Polish. It was just the
country where I was born.

My dad's best friend owned a soap factory and
lived directly above our apartment. Their daughter Mania was my sister's best friend. Dad and Mania's dad
would drink coffee and listen to news on the radio. Hitler was kicking Polish Jews out of Germany and Dad
helped three of these refugees find a place to stay. My
uncle Isaac lived in Germany. He could tell what was
coming and moved to England. He kept urging my father to come with him but Dad said everything would
blow over.

I had no idea what was going on. At sixteen you
walk past nightclubs and wonder when you'll finally be
able to go out dancing. Once in a while we would go
into downtown Krakow to visit the dress shop owned
by my mother's younger sister. She looked like a super-

*model, tall and skinny, blond hair and blue eyes. She
always wore gorgeous clothes and broad-brimmed hats.
This woman was my idol.*

*Basically I was still a child. My main interest in
life was probably the powdered sugar napoleons at the
restaurant across the street. Dad's customers always
gave him samples and one night he came home with a
huge box of chocolate-covered cherries from Suchard's,
the gourmet chocolatier. Mom locked this in a cabinet
but I found the key and ate every one. Before the invasion, that stomach ache was the biggest trauma in my
life.*

The Schiff family lives half a mile from the Baums, on
Krakow Street near the Jewish Community Center. They
don't have it quite as easy. Up on the third floor of a big gray
housing block the five family members share two bedrooms
and a large kitchen. The whole family shares a bathroom with
the Applebaums next door. The Schiffs' kitchen serves as dining room, family room, and conference room. According to
William, the middle child, money discussions frequently required encryption.

*When my parents wanted to keep secrets from us they
spoke Yiddish. Dad was a terrible businessman so we
heard a lot of Yiddish. At one point my father and his
partner had two barber-beauty shops and we lived in a
much nicer apartment. Then he made some bad deals
and lost his partner. We ended up with the smaller shop
and had to move into the little place on Krakow Street.
He had four employees and five chairs in this shop. I*

swept the floors when I was young to help out.

Dad had been a medic in the army of the Austro-Hungarian monarch in World War One. He trained as a corpsman and learned to dress wounds. I was born right after the war. What can I say? I grew up in a family where the woman was the smart one and the man wouldn't listen. I loved my father but I never really liked him a whole lot. When I was six I wanted to buy some candy and he wouldn't give me a nickel. After I cried for two days he finally gave in. I was so excited running to the store I tripped and the nickel fell in the gutter and went down the sewer. Our whole relationship was kind of like that.

My mother I loved dearly. She and I had to scramble to get the family finances back on track. She ran the shop and Dad just cut hair. My older sister Dorothy was studying to be a pharmacist. To help pay her tuition I quit school at fourteen and got a job in a sewing machine repair shop. Over the next six years I also became a bicycle mechanic and learned how to fix radios in the same shop. I was fascinated by radio technology and started taking night school classes. When I was eighteen I was making ten zloties a week and giving most of it to my mom. This was more money than my uncles were making. My younger brother Bronek helped Dad at the shop.

I couldn't afford to be full-time sports crazy like other kids, but working in a bicycle shop you couldn't avoid sports. In Poland at that time bicycle racing was like football and baseball and basketball combined. I did road races with a Jewish club called Maccabi and won a few events. When I turned sixteen I discovered girls and it was bye-bye bicycles.

Throughout my childhood I had always been painfully shy around girls. My sister saw how pathetic I was and said, "William, let me teach you how to dance." She was a phenomenal dancer and after a few years I got very good at classic styles like the tango, foxtrot, and paso doble.

Dorothy and I would save our money, dress up, and go dancing with older friends at popular spots like The Gypsy Club. We thought we were Fred Astaire and Ginger Rogers and we could clear the dance floor when we felt like showing off. I could sing, too, so things started to open up for me socially and I was dating a lot.

That was my life when the Germans seized our city. I was just an average guy. I worked all day fixing bikes and radios, studied electronics at night, and chased girls on the weekend. We didn't have any money, but I was ambitious and excited about my future.

When the sun goes down on the lovely end-of-summer Thursday the Schiff and Baum families sit down to their dinners. Three hundred miles west of their tables an enormous force is gathering in silence on the German border. After six years in power, Adolf Hitler has completed his plan to invade Poland. While the Schiffs and the Baums sleep, his diplomats publicize the excuses. They claim their army has to cross the border to put down Polish rebel attacks. Nazi intelligence agents have faked the terror incidents, but newspapers and radio stations controlled by the government support the shaky argument for war.

World War Two begins with ultramodern tanks and planes and nihilism. Hitler tells his generals to forget their tradition of fair play. "Operation White" is not about taking ground and capturing flags. Secret units from the SS will be following the tanks. Their initial mission seems straightforward: to occupy local media and political offices and pacify the population. But the ruthless methods of the Death Head Special Forces scandalize several old-school officers.

Most soldiers in the regular army believe that Germany was dishonored by foreign politicians and betrayed by its own liberals twenty years earlier. Many grew up in homes squeezed by a hard economy, especially if their fathers were killed in World War One. They have been trained to view the Polish people as backward and treacherous "semi-Asians" and Eastern Jews as cockroaches.

Older soldiers who started as storm troopers embrace the racial politics of their leaders. Younger boots who came up through the Hitler Youth are even more extreme. They believe the future cannot be built until the present is destroyed. Raised on bonfires and the People's Radio, they have idolized combat all their lives. They are schooled to be dominating, indifferent to pain, and free of tenderness. At fifteen minutes before five o'clock on the first morning of September this bitter generation erupts in rage.

Rosalie's heaven is shattered.

A lot of it is still like a cloud in my mind. Right before the Germans came I had a very vivid dream. In this dream I was looking outside through the keyhole in the front door of our apartment complex. The street was full of dead people. I remember this so well because

I saw my favorite aunt, the beautiful girl who owned the dress shop, lying among the other bodies wearing a fancy hat.

The next day Dad came home early from work and said all the men had been told to evacuate. The Germans were calling everybody terrorists so they could shoot anybody they felt like shooting. Dad told us he loved us and kissed us goodbye. Then he left with his two partners and headed for the Russian border.

We never found out what happened to him. One of the partner's sons told me many years later that he was killed while Russian soldiers were chasing him. My last memory of the man I worshipped are the words he spoke to my mother when he kissed her as he went out the front door. He said, "When will people ever stop hating one another?"

A few days later we heard bombing and the soldiers came marching into the city. I went downstairs with my brother and sister and we walked to the main street to watch the parade. There were heavy tanks and miles of men with scowling faces. They swung their arms and stomped their boots and sang, "Germany! Germany! Number One!" We threw candy, one of the great regrets of my life. If I knew then what I know now it would have been poison.

Rosalie's father and his partners march toward the Russian border. All must go on foot because German bombers have crippled the train system. Once their hard targets are taken out, the Luftwaffe pilots tear into the huge column of men. William is in the thick of things with his father and younger brother.

We all headed for Lvov, a town 160 miles east. Before we even got started my brother was almost arrested by our own soldiers. He didn't want to give them his bicycle. Here come the Germans with a thousand tanks and the Polish army is scavenging bicycles from teenagers.

The first day on the road was not a problem. On the second day it was obvious the Polish air force was out of commission. The sky filled with German planes. Technically, they started bombing us because everybody was running away together and there were a lot of Polish soldiers mixed in with the civilians. The Germans didn't really give a damn. They just wanted to kill as many people as possible.

Wherever you turned there were explosions and horses and carriages full of men falling into craters. One bomb hit a wagon thirty yards in front of us and we got knocked over by all kinds of debris. I ran and looked down in the hole, but everybody was too mangled for me to help. Another bomb landed close behind us and we jumped up and ran. Dad fainted twice and we dragged him off the road into the trees. This went on for ten days and it broke my father psychologically. From that point until his deportation three years later he was pretty much like a little child.

Hitler and Stalin have an agreement on how they intend to divide Poland, but a Russian diplomat in Berlin discovers secret German plans to violate the pact and seize Lvov. To protect his nearby oil reserves Stalin rolls out the Ukrainian Front army. Ten days after the Schiff men leave Krakow they run into a noisy and blinding wall of Soviet armored vehicles.

We had been walking forever and sleeping at night in the woods, eating whatever we could find along the way, usually nothing. When we reached the outskirts of Lvov it was almost midnight. The Russians came charging out in tanks and shined spotlights on us. They said, "Drop your weapons, turn around, and go home."

I was three months shy of twenty-one, the legal age for enlistment. Some Polish soldiers had given me an infantryman's jacket and a rifle anyway. They didn't give me any bullets and that was fine with me. I had never touched a gun before. I took off the jacket, put the rifle down and we marched back 160 miles. It only took us a week to get home because we didn't have to hide from the planes any more.

Dad was hysterical the whole time. He said the Germans were going to kill everybody. Based on his experience in the Austrian army he warned me that the Germans would do whatever their leaders told them. He said, "These people are fanatics and orders are sacred to them. They'd kill their own families if that's what they were told to do."

He begged me to listen to him but I thought he was crazy. I told him they were the most advanced people in the world. They had science, industry, Beethoven, everything. German was the universal cultural language, just like English is today. Who could believe that this sophisticated culture would send its army into a big important city like Krakow to kill a quarter of the population?

He begged me and Mom to sell the shop and sneak back into Russia some other way. My mother was actually packing for the trip one afternoon when I put my foot down. I hated communism and I wasn't going to live in that insane society. I didn't believe in everybody theoretically being equal while a small group of people ran the show. I didn't think that kind of system suited human nature.

Besides, even though everybody was Poland's enemy, the Russians had a special reputation for hating Jews. The Russian troops roughed some of us up outside Lvov, me and my brother included. After that experience I thought we'd be safer with the Germans.

There were other warnings we didn't read properly because we were so used to anti-Semitism. Polish kids had been picking fights with Bronek and me our whole lives. We always fought back because we learned early on that this saved you fights down the road. Two years before the invasion the harassment got much more intense. The Polish leader Edward Smigly-Ridz had an agreement with Hitler that let Germany keep dumping Jews on the border. When the Poles saw their leader turn a blind eye to this persecution, it sanctioned their own prejudice and they started coming after us more aggressively.

Bronek had to quit high school because the Polish kids were picking fights with him every day. Once a month he could handle, not every day. When I got back from Lvov I was walking my mom home from the salon. We passed a street demonstration, some guy yelling about Jews to a crowd of people. My mom said, "Pity

the man who is always right, William. There is nothing
on earth sadder than a fanatic." I met the first German
troops the day after that.

William and a friend are walking in the main square
downtown when three German officers approach. A lieutenant points to the metal "Polish eagle" pin William wears on
his jacket lapel, a gift from an infantryman he made friends
with on the long walk to Lvov. The lieutenant's jacket is the
same field-gray SS style that Hitler wore in the Reichstag the
day he announced the invasion. William is entranced by the
silver skull badge on the officer's hat and impressed with his
Polish language skills.

> *He put his hand on my shoulder and said, "I see you*
> *still have pride in your country even though you lost the*
> *war. Personally, I respect that, but other soldiers in our*
> *army probably won't. If I were you, I wouldn't wear this*
> *little eagle out in public any more."*
>
> *When he asked me where I lived in Krakow I didn't*
> *say Kazimierz. That would have told him right away I*
> *was a Jew. I just said I lived a few blocks from down-*
> *town. We walked around the square with these guys a*
> *few times and when I said goodbye to him in German*
> *he gave me a big smile and shook my hand. I went home*
> *and told my dad I'd just made friends with a German*
> *officer. He looked at me like I'd lost my mind.*

The soldiers may belong to the new paramilitary formation
brought to town by SS Brigade Leader Bruno Streckenbach.
The 400 Death Head war-police in his 1st Special Operation

Group are helping the regular Fourteenth Army maintain order. They do this by assassinating teachers, journalists, politicians, Catholic priests, prominent citizens, and leaders of the Jewish community. The new mobile killing teams are the first phase of a depopulation program that will eventually give birth to big streamlined facilities like Auschwitz.

The SS has gained extraordinary power since it mushroomed from Hitler's bodyguard into Germany's national security apparatus. Streckenbach is a top new enforcer and a hardcore Nazi who began his career as a young head-banging storm trooper in Hamburg. Unswerving commitment to the cause earned him his challenging new job. Berlin wants him to drive Jews out of Krakow using whatever form of intimidation he likes. Stars of David are painted on all Jewish businesses, restaurants, coffee shops, and pushcarts. There is a huge commotion one morning in front of William's apartment building as men are grabbed and loaded onto trucks for forced labor.

> *Dad and I were standing there in the street the first time the Germans came to round up workers. Then I saw the SS lieutenant I met in the square. He was in charge of eight or nine men who were beating people up real bad, hitting them in the face with guns, that kind of thing. I was scared that he'd get angry if he recognized me so I pulled my father back into the crowd. We managed to get on a truck without this guy seeing us.*
>
> *That first day we cleaned streets together. I ended up pulling four shifts a week to cover the two shifts Dad was supposed to work. Work was not the point. The point was to mock us and degrade us. "Get a*

broom, Jew! Sweep, Jew, sweep!" Dad couldn't han-
dle it.

I cleaned streets and shoveled snow for months.
Later they sent me to do rock-breaking up on Jaguski
Hill. In the quarries it was the same mind game. They
made us fill hopper wagons with heavy rocks and push
them from one area to another all day long. The next
day they'd order us to move the same rocks back to the
original location. Just to torment us and laugh at us. It
was dangerous work and I got a finger crushed in the
gear of a hopper wagon. Try doing manual labor with a
broken index finger. It's still crooked today.

A week after I got back from Lvov a friend of mine
invited me to a party. A dance teacher we knew put
these things together. I wasn't keen on the idea because
they were popular with younger kids. After walking 300
miles and being bombed and cleaning streets I didn't
feel like wasting my one night out with a bunch of high
school students. I wanted to go to The Gypsy Club or
some other nice place and dance with grown women.
But my buddy wanted to meet a girl at this party and
he kept bugging me so I went.

Through spotless cobbled streets under heavy black lamps
the two friends walk, each in his one good suit. In the upstairs apartment in Kazimierz they join thirty other Jews and
a dance instructor relishing his role as master of ceremonies.
He keeps the phonograph volume down to avoid attention
from soldiers patrolling outside. Rosalie stands in a corner
with her friend Cesia.

I was still in shock from my dad's disappearance and not in a festive mood. When William and his friend walked in, Cesia swooned. She went on and on about how handsome William was and what a great dancer.

At some point in the evening the dance instructor clapped his hands in the middle of the room. He was a funny guy and he made a very melodramatic announcement. He said, "Gentlemen, gentlemen! It's finally the magic moment—lady's tango time!" This meant girls could ask boys to dance. William had been dancing with another girl all night, so Cesia grabbed my arm and told me to cut in and bring him over so she could meet him. She was my best friend so I went over and asked Mr. Casanova if he wanted to dance.

There were no instant fireworks for William.

I was too dazed and preoccupied. But the next morning the girls came by my dad's shop and all three of us went for a walk in the park. That's when I got my first good look at Rose in broad daylight. She was wearing a blue dress and she had blue eyes and long light brown hair. My God, was she beautiful!

From that day on we were together every minute we could be. Her mother liked me so we started dating right away. They lived across the street from the Maccabi sports center where my bike club used to meet. Her father hadn't come back from Russia and they were all alone just as the Germans were starting to get vicious.

In early December, one of Streckenbach's units, Special
Action Squad 2, carries out the first organized terror action
in Kazimierz, for centuries the cultural and spiritual womb of
the Polish Jews. Rosalie is badly shaken.

> *They burned and looted our synagogues. They stole price-*
> *less old chalices and menorahs and burned torah scrolls*
> *and prayer books in the streets. The soldiers grabbed old*
> *men and cut their beards or set them on fire. It made*
> *me angry because I was raised Orthodox and religion*
> *meant a lot to me.*
>
>   *Some of the soldiers looked very young. I didn't un-*
> *derstand how boys could be so cruel. They had captured*
> *Poland quickly and thought they were invincible. Some*
> *people were hoping England might help us but nothing*
> *happened. At night the Germans would get drunk and*
> *sing the same song over and over again, making fun of*
> *the English leader:*
>
> > *You had no luck in Berlin, Chamberlain!*
> > *You had bad luck with Stalin, Chamberlain!*
> > *Umbrella in your hand,*
> > *You cannot save your land!*
> > *You're no hero! You're no man, Chamberlain!*
>
> *That was our predicament. Chamberlain was in Lon-*
> *don, the Germans were drunk in our streets, and we were*
> *hiding in our houses, peeking out through the curtains.*

A new overlord from Berlin comes to Krakow and takes
over the dragon castle on Wawel Hill. Hans Frank, another

hardnosed patriotic bureaucrat, is the first German Governor General of conquered Poland. Frank is a lawyer and smug. He says, "All I want the Krakow Jews to do is disappear."

He flogs the community with new laws. Kosher meat is suddenly illegal and people are forced to dig ditches on the holiest day of the year. Bank accounts are frozen, safety deposit boxes are rifled and valuables confiscated from homes. Jews can only keep a small amount of cash and are forbidden to own automobiles or to ride public transportation. Schools are closed, pensions cancelled, telephones disconnected, and hospital treatment denied. In addition to the Polish police officers and German soldiers who hassle civilians in the streets, now there is also a special Jewish police force to help impose the laws.

"Not all the Jews were angels," William says. "The good Jewish police were maybe one in two hundred. Most of the rest were just mean sons of bitches. Even the good ones would start pushing you around if they saw a German soldier coming. That's what they were getting paid to do. They were always shaking us down for bribe money. If you didn't give them something they could report you as a troublemaker and you might not see your next birthday."

Official identification papers become the key to every Jew's existence. With a job a person can get an ID; without one he or she is doomed. In May 1940, the General Government warns all Jews without identification that they have three months to leave town voluntarily. Too few leave to suit the Germans so Frank issues an eviction notice in November. People caught with no ID will be deported. William has been dating Rosalie for a year when this order threatens their relationship.

Suddenly my girlfriend is an illegal alien in the city
where she was born and raised. Every day you felt more
helpless. They kept tightening the net and the mood in
the street kept getting uglier. Rose and I were minding
our own business in the park one day when we walked
past a bench where two Polish guys were sitting. They
thought it would be funny to trip the Jews so they stuck
their feet out and Rose almost fell. They were my age so
I got into it with them. I ended up with black eyes and
a busted lip but I also landed some punches.

Rose was horrified but I wanted to show her how
bullies operate. The next day I took her back to the same
park and deliberately walked her past the same two guys.
She was surprised when they pretended not to see me and
let us go quietly by. The only reason I mention this juve-
·nile incident is because it was the last fair fight I had in
Europe. After that we'd be walking down the street and
the Polish kids would point us out to the Germans and
yell: "Hey, here's some Jews! Shoot them!" They weren't
kidding, and Jews were getting shot.

One year after the invasion Rosalie is seventeen, William
twenty-one. They must wear white armbands on their right
sleeve with a blue Star of David and are forbidden to walk
in the parks. Nobody feels like dancing or singing and sugar-
dusted napoleons are a thing of the past. William's father's
spirits continue to deteriorate. With blood in the streets it's
not surprising the former medic doesn't feel like cutting hair.
It would be better for his family if he chose not to stay in the
apartment and cry all day.

Prospects aren't any brighter in Rosalie's home, even

though her dad left her mom with money. "William wouldn't take money from us," she says, "because in our culture it was a man's job to provide. Women were just for making babies. That sounds insulting, I know, but if a trendy person today went back in a time machine to Poland sixty years ago it would seem like six hundred years. My mother had been shielded from any kind of responsibility and she was completely disoriented. It was also at this time she discovered she had a large tumor in a breast and needed surgery. So William felt doubly obligated."

With the parks and sidewalks off limits and their homes full of sorrow the couple take brief furtive walks when they can. It's the only way to savor each other's company. If invaders appear with grinning skulls on their uniforms the lovers instinctively look down and pass meekly. Tonight they walk to the river. There is moonlight on the Vistula, always a pleasant thing to ponder.

William walks Rosalie home past the castle. On the other side of the wall Hans Frank is finishing dinner with the man who will destroy their lives. Over cognac and coffee Frank mulls the fate of the Krakow Jews with Heinrich Himmler, the SS National Leader. With his small head and spectacles, Himmler is nothing like the tall Nordic warriors filling the new SS army. The former chicken farmer has never fired a shot in battle, but he has arranged enough deaths to make himself the second most powerful man in the Reich and master of many new secret prisons. Perching his demitasse spoon on a gold-rimmed saucer, he reaches across the tablecloth to tap his cigar on a triangular black marble ashtray.

On the doorstep of 7 Dietlovska Street, a bicycle repairman gives a good night kiss to the oldest daughter of Benzion Baum, formerly one of the best-respected businessmen in Krakow.

chapter two

"In this ghetto we were married"

Amber was big business in Poland long before the country had a name. Primitive people thought the sunshine-colored tree resin they dug up out of the ground could bring them luck and make them young again. When Roman nobles started buying the pretty stuff, the Vistula was already part of the "amber road" that carried Mediterranean and Byzantine traders north to the main deposits on the Baltic coast.

Some of these men were Jews who noticed that locals on the southern banks of the river mined salt, another valuable commodity. A few merchants settled in the convenient town that began to gather around Wawel Hill. Other Jewish settlers in Krakow worked the trade route between Provence and eastern outposts that would eventually bloom as Prague and Kiev.

In the Middle Ages more Jews arrived, fleeing countries where the Crusades had whipped commoners into anti-Semitic frenzies. There were waves of refugees when Jews were blamed for the bubonic plague and later during the Inquisition. Friction with the native population was a given. Eight hundred years before the Nazis came to Krakow, a teacher protested that city authorities had no right to punish his students for beating up residents of Jew Street. Most locals considered that kind of behavior good clean fun and a normal rite of passage for high-spirited Christian boys.

King Casimir the Great was more enlightened. He welcomed Jewish artisans and let the brilliant Krakow banker Lewko run the royal mint and modernize the economy. As the Jewish community flourished, success created resentment. In 1407, a preacher at St. Anne's Church initiated a major hate riot. Jews were murdered and their homes ransacked until the governor sent in armed troops.

Jews were also blamed repeatedly for fires that broke out in the city's ramshackle wooden neighborhoods. After a devastating blaze in 1494, the entire Jewish population was driven from Krakow into Kazimierz, at that time a township on an island in the Vistula. Here they continued to weave fabric, publish books, and expand their trade throughout the region. Among the goods were salt, honey, wax, fish, dried fruit, skins, needles, and ribbons. As decades passed the mix would include silk, vodka, saffron, lemons, and hats made of gray squirrel fur.

A wall was built in 1608 to isolate the Jews from the Christian population. The wall was torn down in 1822 to force the Jews to assimilate. Hans Frank, the new Nazi governor of Krakow, announces another wall on March 3, 1941. A ghetto will be built in a neighborhood called Podgorze. Christians living in the designated area have two weeks to get out. The Jews have two weeks to get in and anyone who refuses risks deportation. The threat shakes William.

We woke up one morning and the big news is the ghetto. Everybody was losing their minds with panic and speculation. The Germans decided who got to stay and started handing out passes. My poor dad was crying extra hard because he knew what they had in mind. Rose's mom didn't get a pass either because she never worked a day in her life. She was lost in a world where everyone was looking out for himself. All the male relatives who kissed up to her when her husband was in the picture suddenly had no time to help.

Residents of Kazimierz gather belongings, cross a Vistula bridge, and walk through a tall gate manned by Polish and German guards. Inside the new high-walled corral more than 15,000 people crowd into 320 houses. Thanks to a year of street cleaning, snow shoveling, and rock breaking without pay, William has an ID and manages to secure a fairly decent flat for the Schiffs. It is one-third the size of the apartment on Krakow Street but at least they have it to themselves.

None of the Baums qualifies for the magic paperwork. Forced to abandon their comfortable lodgings, Rosalie and her family join thousands of others seeking refuge in the countryside.

William found us a place in a little town called Pro-kochim. He rented a wagon and we loaded up a few essentials. He pushed while Mom and my sister Lucy and I took turns pulling. Everything in the country was blooming and looked beautiful as the Germans started to make Krakow "Jew-free." This was a top priority for the new capital of the General Government. We were like garbage that had to be swept away so the city would be clean for the new owners.

We walked down the road together. Lucy was silent after saying goodbye to her best friend Mania who lived upstairs. I hate to remember those two young girls hugging and crying. My brother Henry was completely confused. Like all young kids he was intensely curious about the world and he kept asking me why we had to leave our home. What was I supposed to tell him? How could an eight year-old understand the concept "Jew-free?"

Nobody understood what was happening. One morning you'd wake up and the Germans would say everybody has to move over here. The next morning you wake up and it's another major reshuffle. It was maddening.

We ended up on a farm in an old wooden shelter with holes in the roof and bad sanitary conditions. Mom and Lucy got typhus right away and I had to nurse them through that. Typhus was common in Poland and Russia. I had never seen it before so I was scared to death when they broke out with the dark spots. During one night of really high fever mom kept talking about my dad. For a few hours she thought I was my dad.

We would have all starved to death without the extra food William brought us. To make these deliveries he had to take off his Star of David armband, sneak out of the ghetto and walk several miles on roads patrolled by German soldiers. This was a serious violation of the racial laws, punishable by death.

In the food rationing system established by Frank, Germans in the General Government are each allowed 2,600 calories a day. Poles are granted 700 and Jews get 184. Before long the Reich's Statistical Office in Berlin is using IBM punch cards to factor the starvation death rate per square kilometer. William has to rack his brain to feed nine mouths.

Nobody could live on the rations. I went from making great money in the repair shop to working for free. So I had to sell clothes in the street. After the Germans took our businesses and our jobs, clothes were all we had left.

In those days no one had as many outfits as the average person today. If you had two suits you were a rich man. So the Poles were thrilled when the Jews had to dump all this high-quality apparel. And they got it for nothing. I'd pull together what I could and hustle outside cafes. "Look, mister, what a beautiful pair of shoes! Only two loaves of bread!" It was never enough. The new laws were designed to kill us so we had to break them. If you didn't smuggle or organize, your family would starve. "Organizing" is a nice word for stealing.

My labor detail changed from the quarry to a nail factory in town. It was the usual robot assignment: "Here, Jew, separate the big nails from the little nails." I did this all day long and another worker asked me to help him smuggle aluminum strips out so he could resell them back in town. We did this maybe half a dozen times but I had a bad feeling about it right from the start.

There was a Polish foreman in the plant who didn't like me. You couldn't buck these guys any more because

now there were German soldiers everywhere looking
for any excuse to shoot a Jew. This particular foreman
loved the fact that we were helpless. He antagonized us
all day long and he knew it drove me crazy.

One day after my partner slipped me the aluminum the foreman stopped me walking out the door. He
threw me against the wall to frisk me and he was gloat-
ing because he knew he had me. He said, "You're dead,
Jew."

He patted down every inch of my body including
the back hip area where I tucked the strips. He patted
to the right of them, to the left, just above and just
below. Then he did it again. To this day I have no idea
how he could miss them a second time. When I gave the
metal to my partner that night I told him that was my
last run. I couldn't help Rose if I was dead.

There was a section of the ghetto wall some friends
of mine and I climbed over a few nights until some other guys got shot doing the same thing. From then on if
you wanted out you had to bribe the gate guards. I paid
them off twice a week so I could take Rose whatever
food I scrounged up. They made a fortune off smugglers
and I had to deny myself everything to see her. I was so
in love I didn't care.

What I needed was a better way to get food. One
day I was walking back into the city and I saw this little
white shed back up under a cluster of shade trees. An
old Polish woman came out holding a live chicken upside down and she waved goodbye to somebody inside.
I stopped and walked over. Inside there was a very old
farmer, a little stooped-over man with no teeth. He says,

"What can I sell you today, sir?"

The shed was full of buckets of butter and cheese and eggs. A dozen live chickens were hanging upside down from the ceiling. I couldn't believe it. A mile and a half away in the ghetto Jews were starting to die from hunger. I ran back to the ghetto to tell my mom. She had such a capable mind I knew she'd figure out a way for me to sneak food past the guards.

She gave me my father's best coat and told me to trade it on the streets for the biggest overcoat I could find. When I came back with a huge brown coat she was rigging flour sacks to a belt. Two in front, one on each side, one in the back. The sacks were for chickens and she warned me to put the birds in upside down. For some reason when you turn a chicken upside down it stops making noise. This was important because a noisy chicken would mean a bullet in the head.

Orthodox Jews like William's mother can only eat chickens that have been killed by a studied and recognized ritual slaughterer. Because a dead animal was considered unclean and inedible, the chickens have to be smuggled into the ghetto alive.

Two or three times a week I dressed up in torn pants and the sloppy coat. Soldiers didn't hassle me any more because I looked like a beggar and Krakow was now full of beggars. My first run was a disaster. I'd never bought a chicken before and the old farmer sold me scrawny birds no one wanted. When I got back and laid them out on the table in the kitchen everybody looked

at me like I was an idiot. The next time I had to pay the
guards double so mom could sneak out to the shed with
me. She showed me where to touch a chicken to make
sure it was nice and fat.

People came to our apartment to trade for the
chickens. Everybody was starving and nobody had any
money or any clothes left. You want to help everybody
but you can't. Mom would give chickens to her Orthodox friends. She said we had to be merciful to them
because they were good religious people. When I asked
where their mercy was the day I bought the skinny chickens she slapped me. A couple times I told her I wasn't
going out any more. It was too stressful. If the Germans
hear a bird they shoot you. If they catch you without
your armband they shoot you.

I tried taking my brother out with me and a few
times we got back with ten birds. But one day we passed
three German soldiers and he acted real nervous. That
day we almost both got shot. Bronek would do anything
I asked him to do but he was not a smuggler. It was too
hard on his nerves.

At this stage the Germans were getting to all of
us psychologically. One time I went out and the shed
was closed. The farmer had put a sign up: "Working
land, back in two hours." I waited seven hours before
he showed up and it was very late when I finally got
back with a large load. In the dark out in front of our
apartment I almost didn't recognize my mother. Her
hair seemed so much grayer and her cheeks were hollow.
When I went back out again the next day she put her
head down on the table and cried. But she didn't say a

word. What could she say? My father was crying in the other room and we had to feed him somehow.

In the densely overcrowded ghetto there is little coal or wood for warmth. German terror teams keep kicking doors, subjecting women to "gynecological examinations" and breaking fingers when they steal rings. Where there is room to walk in the street pedestrians step over corpses, some with faces too badly pulped to identify. The SS has been sending in savage Ukrainian auxiliaries for round-ups, kidnappings, and liquidations. William assumes these "Black Uniforms" kill his uncle, one of countless citizens who mysteriously disappear. Into this pandemonium another proclamation from Hans Frank herds 3,000 Jews from the countryside, Rosalie and her family among them.

We woke up out on the farm and they told us to move back to Krakow. Back to the city they just kicked us out of. Somehow William found a place for us in a one-room apartment in the ghetto. I have tried to forget this place for sixty years. It had no windows and no heat. Mother, Lucy, Henry, and I had one corner and eight other people divided the rest. Nobody had a job and it was too dangerous to go outside so everybody sat on the floor all day long crying from hunger.

My mother found a doctor to remove her breast, but the Germans had confiscated all the anesthesia. So my brother and sister and I stood outside this ghetto office listening to Mom scream. A few weeks later my sister and I took the sutures out ourselves, again without anesthesia.

In the summer of 1942 the SS has its first death camps
up and running. It's time to empty the Polish ghettos of every
Jew who cannot be used as a work slave. In the Schiff family
William has his job, Dorothy is a licensed pharmacist, and
Bronek is a healthy young male ripe for exploitation. Bertha
and Michael have no excuse and William can't protect his
parents from soldiers waving pistols.

> *When they came into the apartment to take them I
> said, "Either we all go or nobody goes." The four Ger-
> mans just laughed and pushed me into a corner. Mom
> told me to take care of my brother and sister. I slipped
> her what little money I had. Then the soldiers marched
> them to the train. Mom said she'd get in touch with me
> as soon as they settled into their new life and new jobs
> in the Ukraine. Those are the last words I heard her
> say. "I'll contact you as soon as I can." Dad just cried
> and hung on her arm.*

The deportations go on all week. On the final day William stands beside his girlfriend while armed men take her
family. June 7, 1942, is the worst day of Rosalie's life.

"The Germans came pounding on the door of this night-
mare room," she says, "My baby brother was hanging on my
legs because the shouting scared him. He asked me why he
couldn't stay. I told him: 'Honey, you don't have permission.'"

In the middle of the room Helena Baum holds a small
suitcase containing socks and underwear for the youngsters.
She wears a coat with gold coin buttons that will end up in
Berlin with other loot from the dead. Still weak from her

mastectomy, she ignores as long as possible the shouts of two steel-helmeted Waffen SS infantry men. She has a covenant to arrange with William.

> *We heard a rifle outside the door—loud—and a woman shrieking in the street because the Germans just shot her son. Rose's mom didn't even blink. She said, "William, you know I like you, but I can't leave my daughter here with you unless you promise me you'll marry her. There has to be a proper wedding with a rabbi and someone from city hall. And you have to give me your word you won't touch her until after the ceremony."*
>
> *I said, "Sure, Mrs. Baum, I give you my word."*
> *She said, "All right, then, Rose, you can stay."*
> *Then the Germans grabbed her and pushed her out the door with the kids.*

In the next raid on the ghetto William's brother Bronek is caught walking the streets without his ID and deported. So is Zofi, the shy fifteen-year-old cousin who always begged William to sing at family functions. For safety's sake Rosalie moves into William's apartment.

"She slept with my sister and I slept in the front room. Ten days later we got married the way her mom wanted. We didn't have any nice linen so strangers raised a rag up over our heads in this same apartment. The rabbi said what he said. We said what we had to say. That was it—man and wife. I was twenty-three. Rose was nineteen. Somebody found a half bottle of wine so I drank a toast and broke the glass. We were all wondering how we were going to stay alive."

Rosalie would prefer not to say her vows in old borrowed clothes, but is grateful for the presence of the rabbi from her father's synagogue.

He did his best to cheer everybody up. He said, "O, our friend Baum's little daughter is getting married! How can I marry such a baby?" My grandmother Sarah and William's sister were the only other people I knew in the room.

I found my grandmother wandering the streets after the Germans took the aunt she lived with, the one who owned the dress shop and loved fancy hats. Sarah was a sweet old lady, in shock and very confused. She had been hiding in alleys and doorways while the soldiers killed people. This is the woman who sang me to sleep with old lullabies every night when I was a baby. She was a very devout person who never put a crumb in her mouth without first saying a blessing.

After the wedding I hid her in the attic above the apartment. The Germans kept raiding and killing and I wanted to make sure they didn't get her. She was the only family I had left. When we thought danger was coming I would tell her to lie flat on the floor in a corner and not move or cough. Then I would cover her with newspapers. That sounds stupid, I'm sure, but I couldn't think of anything better.

The last time I saw her she told me she didn't want me to save her any more. She said she was old already and her sore foot hurt a lot and she was tired of being hungry. I went out and begged for a slice of bread so she could eat something. A slice of bread was like a million

dollars and it took me hours to find one. When I came
back with the food she was gone.

For two days I literally could not speak. I was an
orphan now and completely in shock from all the chaos
around us. William helped me get ahold of myself. He
knew the Germans would get me next if I didn't.

During the June terror in the ghetto, 300 Jews are shot
dead and 6,000 shipped east to the Belzec death camp. All
are offloaded, gassed with carbon monoxide, and cremated.
Among them are Sarah, Helena, Lucy, Henry, Bertha, Michael, Bronek, and Zofi. In Krakow, people continue to believe their deported relatives are safe. William wholeheartedly
believes his parents have been sent to the Ukraine to begin
new jobs in war factories.

"That's what the Germans told us. Nobody thought they'd
murder everyone. Even after they put us through three years
of hell and made us live in the ghetto it was still inconceivable.
But the day they took Rose's family I saw soldiers shoving children onto a transport train. One of them kicked a little girl so
hard he could have broken her back. That gave me a real bad
feeling. So almost three years after the invasion my eyes finally
started to open. It was way too late to do anything then."

In July William gets a letter from the dead. A gentile woman delivers a folded piece of paper to the main ghetto gate,
something Zofi passed to her at Belzec. William stands by the
gate absorbing his cousin's girlish handwriting. She says that
when Bronek stepped down from the boxcar the SS guards
motioned him into the group of men selected to live. Bronek
didn't read the situation correctly and assumed that the men
in this group were about to be shot. When the guards weren't

looking, he snuck back into the mass of people chosen for death. A verbatim translation:

"He thought they took him to shoot, so he smuggled himself into the fire."

William stares at the blue-black calligraphy on paper blazing white in the sun. In the loopy script the word "fire" stands out starkly. Tucking the letter into his jacket pocket he hurries back to the apartment to check on his wife. Whatever this fire might be he knows it took a miracle to keep her out of it. Rosalie is still amazed by her good luck.

> *I was in Peace Square waiting in a long line the day before they took my family. I was going to beg for some little job to save my neck. The Germans had just made their final announcement: get a stamp on your card or else. I was standing there and out of nowhere a man walked up in a tailored tan suit and matching hat. He looked at me and said, "You are much too pretty to be in this line."*
>
> *He walked me to the front of the line and told a soldier to give me a work permit. The soldier stamped my card without saying a word. Then the man smiled and walked away. I didn't have time to thank him or even think to beg him to do the same thing for my mom and sister. Who had ever heard of Oskar Schindler back then? May his name be blessed.*

With their parents gone, William guards his bride warily.

> *A girl we knew was raped by ten Black Uniforms and the Germans were coming into the ghetto just to kill.*

They would stand over a body and watch the blood pour out and laugh. One day they made a stack of bodies four feet high. Finally they made the ghetto smaller and started to rampage, hunting and slaughtering people every day. It was awful then. We had no food, nothing.

Even before the wild killing started people had been disappearing for three years. So every day for three years you'd be tying your shoes thinking, "Is today my last day?" Imagine a thousand days in a row like that. Sometimes you thought it would be a big relief to get shot. At least then you wouldn't have to worry any more.

When the Poles saw how the soldiers were victimizing us they piled on, too. One day a German guard was marching me and some other men to the nail factory. At the main gate a Polish boy ran up out of nowhere and stabbed me in the hand with a pocket knife. Not a huge blade, but he sank it all the way into the back of the hand I hurt in the quarry.

My hand was bleeding a lot and I tried to wrap it with a handkerchief. The little Polish kid and the big German guard stood there laughing. "Ha, ha, damn Jew!" That was the atmosphere in the streets. That was the day I stopped trusting everybody. They'd march me to the factory in the morning and I'd sort the stupid nails all day, terrified that Rose or Dorothy would be gone when I got back. Or both of them. It was in this ghetto, this madhouse, we were married.

As Christmas nears in 1942 Krakow is full of Germans doing last-minute shopping before they head home for the holidays. As usual, a large number of officers are hanging out at The Gypsy Club. The party ends abruptly on December 22 when Jewish resistance fighters throw half a dozen hand grenades between the tables. Seven Germans die and many are wounded. Sirens wail as military vehicles speed the corpses through the streets. When word of the attack reaches the ghetto, Rosalie is not surprised.

> *I heard someone shout, "The Gypsy Club's been blown up! The resistance has struck back!" My first reaction was, "Good job, Shimon and Syzmek!" I grew up next door to the Draenger brothers. They had run off to the woods to put together the partisan movement that operated out of a bunker on Skavinska Street. I remember a song people were singing after these brave boys struck back:*
>
> > *We Jews, we're not dead yet!*
> > *God is over us! God is over us!*
> > *Hitler will end up hanging upside down.*
> > *Good health to him and cholera, too!*
> > *We'll slice him into little pieces!*
>
> *It broke our hearts when the Draengers were executed.*

In the spring of 1943 the Krakow ghetto is no longer needed. All across conquered Poland Heinrich Himmler is emptying these temporary holding pens and relocating all the work slaves who survived the liquidations to permanent camps in the countryside. William can picture quite clearly the day he and his wife began their journey.

"Nice spring day, about seventy degrees. They gathered us one morning and marched us down the road. Men in one group, women in another. The camp was just a few miles away, in a suburb past the little shed where I traded for chickens."

After a woman who stumbles is shot, Rosalie keeps her eyes on the ground and watches her steps carefully. Walking away from the city of her youth, she doesn't think about the school where she liked to study history or the hat-loving aunt who is now ashes. Instead, she struggles with visions from the morning of the cruelest terror action. The Death Head troops outdid themselves that day.

> *I had just bartered a dress for some bread at a friend's apartment. When I was walking back I turned the corner and heard shots and screaming. There was a crowd watching soldiers in the middle of the street. The soldiers were shooting up at strange objects flying through the air. These were children that other soldiers were throwing out of the windows on the third floor of an orphanage.*
>
> *The soldiers in the street shot the children as they fell. If they weren't dead when they landed, the soldiers picked them up by the feet and swung them against a wall to break their heads. There was so much blood in the gutter. I saw little eyes, little arms, little insides. I went home and screamed and screamed.*
>
> *"The world is crazy! There is no God! I don't believe in human beings!"*

chapter three

Plaszow: The first camp

In a valley between two sterile hills a hulking man stands on a gallows. He fills a meticulously tailored gray uniform with a high black collar. A silver eagle and skull adorn his hat. Six-foot four without the hat, he is not dwarfed by three noosed men standing on chairs beside him. The giant glares down from his platform at thousands of prisoners in geometric array. It's showtime for Storm Captain Amon Leopold Goeth.

"You've all been warned many times before," he shouts. "You break the rules, you get what you deserve."

The baritone bounces off the hastily built wooden barracks flanking the broad dirt square. This is the roll-call assembly yard, where justice is always loud and one-sided. The men with rope around their necks have been accused of sabotage. The charge can mean escape, smuggling, possession of valuables, disobeying an order—anything the guards please. A piece of salami in your pocket is flagrant sabotage.

The Storm Captain considers himself an athlete, but he has gone to seed during his tenure as commandant of Forced Labor Camp Plaszow. An alcoholic and caffeine junkie, he has a gut and breasts that bounce up and down when he rides his horse hard. His jowly, wattled face is lobster-red today.

He reaches over to a phonograph on a small table and drops the needle on a wax platter. The witty, elegant notes of "The Bat" by Johann Strauss the Younger swell through pole-top speakers and the waltz reverberates against the slopes that frame the 200-acre compound. When the chairs are yanked away two men kick and go purple. The third hits the gallows deck hard. Stunned and bloody-nosed, the fallen prisoner is quickly renoosed and three grunting Death Head soldiers manually hoist him high.

When Goeth pulls his pistol to put a hole in each head, a prisoner in the front row of spectators tries to look down. One of the giant's troops lifts the chin back up with a bayonet. The blade draws blood on William's throat.

> We had to watch. They wanted us to see it all and be terrified. That was the whole point. Nine times out of ten at Plaszow they'd shoot you wherever you were standing the minute they said you broke a rule. But the main yard was an orderly place where we assembled every morning and evening to be counted. To show us that no place was normal or safe they deliberately rubbed death in our faces here. At least once a week they made people dig their own graves on the edges of the yard. Then they'd line them up and shoot them in front of us.
>
> They warned us the first day that if anybody escaped they'd kill every member of his family in the camp. Plus fifty innocent strangers. The next day a friend of mine escaped and we watched his family and

*fifty other people dig their own graves. So for a lot of us
the electric fence wasn't the real barrier to freedom.*

*They let me keep my job in the nail factory in Kra-
kow and marched me back and forth every day. This
was good luck. I could try to cut deals with the Polish
workers for food to smuggle back to Rose and my sister.
Once in a while one of the Poles might share a piece
of herring with you at lunch. Any stray scrap of food
helped fend off the hunger pangs.*

Shortly after his internment William is recruited to join
the Jewish police, a job with big advantages. These privileged
prisoners live in a private barrack with their families in rooms
that lock from the inside. While others wither away on water broth and sawdust bread, policemen get double rations of
thick soup and proper loaves with jam. In exchange for these
perks they are issued whips and expected to use them.

As chief of the Jewish police, Willek Chilowicz is Goeth's
trusted flunky and partner in the black market that develops in every camp where prisoners are stripped of valuables.
Chilowicz and his wife Marysia are loathed for their lordly
pretensions and insensitivity to the suffering of the general
population. William knows both of them well.

*Before I met Rose I went out on a few dates with Mary-
sia. I thought she was a nice girl but when I told her
I didn't want to see her any more she got pretty upset.
Chilowicz was older than me and friends with a very
good friend of mine, a guy I'd known since first grade. It
was this buddy who approached me and basically said,
"Hey, you need to get on the force with us. At least that*

way you know that you and Rose will come out of this thing alive."

I said thanks but no thanks. I didn't like the idea of beating up people I was raised with. The next thing I know here comes Mietek Finkelstein, the top intimidator for Chilowicz. He had no problem with beating people up. Mietek would kill you if he thought he had to.

"William," he says, "I hear you don't want to join the force. Are you crazy, or do you think you're too good to be a cop?"

This was the last guy I needed as an enemy. I told him I knew it was an honor and an important job, but I didn't think I'd be any good at it. He saw right through me and said, "Well, you had your chance."

Everybody was trying to figure out how to save themselves and their kids and survival instinct made the cops take the bait. When you are being beaten every day and somebody suddenly says that will stop, it sounds pretty good. No more hunger, nobody will shoot you. It sounds like a hell of a deal. In the end Goeth shot all these guys and their families, too, just to make sure they didn't talk.

My cop buddy helped get Rose off a few bad work crews. The option wasn't available very often but I used it every time I could. One day I found out she'd been assigned to a crew that moved real heavy lumber all day. My buddy was ready to help but Mietek found out and wouldn't let him. The next time I saw Mietek he said, "I told you, William, you had your chance."

Goeth rents twenty-eight long wooden warehouses inside the fence to businesses. Professors from Krakow's Jagellonian

University find themselves stuffing seagrass into mattresses for German soldiers. Lawyers, rabbis, and poets crank out brushes, locks, shoes, clothing, furniture, and furs at gunpoint. Jewish women are harnessed like draft horses to stone carts in the two camp quarries. With her protection cancelled, Rosalie has to carry lumber.

"It was a work camp and they promised if we did our jobs we'd be okay," she says. "So we had hope until Goeth arrived and started working us to death. Nonstop for twelve-hour shifts we carried big beams back and forth from the railway cars to the sites. A lot of us got hernias and many collapsed and were shot."

When Goeth takes control of the camp he does so with a tacky splash. Exhausted and starving in the three-tiered bunks that line the walls of each long barrack, the Krakow Jews are awakened late one night by music and loud laughter from the white house on a ledge overlooking the camp. Squeezing out over two other girls on her hard bed shelf, Rosalie walks over to a window and looks up at German officers dancing on the balcony of the commandant's villa with their wives and hooker escorts.

"They were dancing, we were dropping dead. He announces himself with this fiesta and the next day he was out on the same balcony shooting down into the camp and killing innocent people. We were all afraid to look up at the white house for fear of a bullet between the eyes. When William and I visited Plaszow several years ago I was still afraid to look up. Goeth had been dead for sixty years."

Storm Captain was the most common SS officer rank. Members of the club include Klaus Barbie, the Gestapo "Butcher of Lyon," and Josef Mengele, the "Angel of Death" at Auschwitz. Early in his career Goeth was nicknamed "The Bloody Dog of Lublin." Rosalie styles him more plainly.

> *The worst experience my family suffered at the hands of this Nazi pig was the senseless murder of my cousin Nucia. So cute, so sweet, ten years old. In addition to Polish she was already fluent in German and French. She might have been a genius. Goeth came up to her one day and took out his revolver and pointed it at her head right in front of her mother.*
>
> *Nucia held up her arms and begged him, "Please don't shoot me. I can peel potatoes. I can clean dishes in the kitchen. I can do a lot of things." He laughed and shot her. Then he told my aunt to get back to work. She never recovered. How could she?*

Handsome Ralph Fiennes scored an Oscar nomination for his icy portrayal of the villain of *Schindler's List*. Under the microscope the real man is more troubling. Oskar Schindler's wife Emelie marveled at his two personalities, one charming, the other the most despicable she ever saw.

The Storm Captain grew up in an affluent middle-class Catholic home in Vienna. His father published military and business books. When Hitler attacked Poland, Goeth was a thirty-one-year-old publisher and new father himself. He liked to talk about music, poetry, and chess, but his real passion was war.

Inspired by a wild friend in the Hitler Youth he entered the Nazi world at seventeen. The plunge into right-wing politics alarmed his liberal workaholic parents and that was the purpose of the exercise. Goeth resented them for shorting him on time and affection. When he joined the SS five years later he told friends the joy of camaraderie drew him into the elite guard service. A more electric thrill was getting paid to break the law. Despite his professed respect for regulations he was immersed in covert actions from the start. He smuggled weapons, money, and intelligence in and out of Austria for Berlin. When Hitler prepared to seize Austria, Goeth had a hand in the terror bombings, assassinations, and other destabilization efforts that paved the way.

When war breaks out he serves as a death-camp construction inspector and then becomes an expert in deportation and liquidating ghettos. He excels as a logistics administrator and defense contract negotiator. Superior officers praise his courage, intelligence, determination, flawless manners, and the soundness of his character and political sensibilities. His perfectionism shows in every document, every manicured nail. At age thirty-five he takes charge of Plaszow. By now the pompous, unloved college dropout is also a serial killer.

Like many modern war criminals he will argue that the enemy of his people had no human or legal rights. He insists that the death and torture he dispensed in his secret eastern prison were required by military emergency, not fueled by hate. This noble pose is contradicted by prisoners who saw him shoot a woman for smiling and make a sick child eat its own diarrhea. He urinates on corpses, shoots secretaries for typos, chefs if his soup is too hot, window washers who miss a spot, and a kennel worker his dogs seem to like more than they fancy their master. He loves to watch these dogs tear men apart, one of the grislier spectacles Rosalie endures one afternoon.

"To this day I can't go anywhere near a big dog," she says.

Train after train offloads Jews from all across Poland and neighboring countries at the railway spur inside the main gate.

More than 150,000 will funnel through Plaszow; 22,000 will die
there. The quickening pace of operations forces Goeth to thin
the herd so ruthlessly prisoners figure their average life-span at
four weeks. He fills many boxcars for the slow day's journey to
Auschwitz and starts hanging women and children. Hangings
become so frequent Rosalie is pulled off the lumber detail and
assigned to "heaven patrol," the worst duty in the camp.

> *My job was to take bodies down from the gallows and
> to pick up the corpses of people who died overnight. Two
> other girls and I took turns pushing and pulling a big
> wooden wheelbarrow. Every morning we loaded it with
> the dead stacked outside the main door of each barrack.
> This was in winter and the bodies were stripped naked
> so other prisoners could keep warm.*
>
> *You tried not to look at the faces, especially the sui-
> cides who grabbed hold of the electrified fence. The first
> day I had to pick up two suicides and the agony was fro-
> zen on their faces. As soon as we filled the cart, armed
> guards escorted us outside the main section of the camp.
> We pushed it up a hill with the wooden wheels creak-
> ing. Once we got to the top we saw a bunch of soldiers
> standing around a big pit full of naked bodies.*

Originally an earthwork fort built ages earlier, this mound
is the camp's main mass murder and burial site. Its ridge en-
circles a deep wide depression and pokes up on the skyline,
visible to all below. The SS men who run the killing there
burn thousands of Jews on layers of logs in the big dirt bowl
on top of the hill.

"A soldier came over to our cart and popped open each
mouth," Rosalie recalls. "They always had a pair of pliers in

their pockets. They would pull out any tooth that had a tiny piece of gold and then tell us to throw the bodies in. I never got used to the sound a body made landing on the big body pile."

William almost ends up in the pit after a scuffle at the nail factory. The day begins normally. After roll call his work detail marches into town and settles into its drudgery. The routine disintegrates when the same foreman who frisked him months earlier begins to beat a young worker. The clubbing intensifies after the worker drops to the floor.

> We saw beatings every day but this was too much. It went on and on. We could tell that the foreman was going to kill the kid, so I finally went over and asked him why he was beating a boy. He said, "Because he's a dirty Jew." I said, "Well, if he's a dirty Jew, then you're a dirty Polack."
>
> I wasn't trying to be brave. But when you're young it's impossible to control your emotions all the time. The foreman got up and threatened me with the club. I said, "If you hit me I'm not going to take it." He slapped me and I knocked him down.
>
> Some other workers came over and the foreman jumped up and started screaming and ringing a bell. Now the Ukrainian Black Uniforms come running in and surrounded everybody. The foreman got on the telephone and called the administrative headquarters up at Plaszow. Twelve or thirteen of us were arrested and sent up to Goeth charged with sabotage. While we were being marched back one of the Ukrainians whispered to me, "Jew, give me everything in your pocket and I'll let you run away."

I said, "If I run away they'll shoot my wife and my
sister and fifty innocent people." He said, "Don't be
stupid, Jew. They're going to shoot everybody up there
anyway. You might as well save your own skin." I told
him I couldn't live with myself if I did such a thing. He
laughed and shook his head.

After the foreman's telephone call, news of the brawl
spreads quickly through the camp. Rosalie has just wheeled
an empty cart down from the pit when word reaches her. "I
heard what happened and was just wild. For a Jew to be accused of sabotage meant I'd probably be rolling William up
the hill before the day was over."

She runs to the fence by the gate with the families of
the other accused men. As the guards march William into
the camp, his wife's face begs for an explanation. "She was
standing there, staring at me through the fence and crying.
I moved my hand across my throat to let her know we were
dead men."

When Rosalie tries to run to her husband her feet fly out
from underneath her as her head snaps back. Landing on her
rear, she looks up into the eyes of the Jewish policeman who
grabbed her hair. The man in the blue cap with the distinctive
yellow stripe drags her back to a barrack, caveman-style. Hands
on hips in the middle of the melee, Mietek Finkelstein orders
police officers to remove sobbing relatives from the scene.

"They wouldn't let me leave the barrack," Rosalie says, "so
I howled for an hour until a friend of mine finally ran in and
said Goeth had let them all off. I didn't believe it. Nobody
could believe it. He had never spared anybody brought up on
appeal before. Especially not for sabotage. William had aston-
ishing luck that day."

A few hours before the nail factory crew arrived for punishment the Plaszow gate guards caught members of another work crew smuggling food. When these men were brought up on appeal, Goeth made their family members dig a huge grave before his Ukrainian troops shot sixty people.

"He must have felt like he'd had enough blood for one day," Rosalie notes. "By the time William's group was brought up he was already drunk and clowning around."

The intoxicated commandant tells the guards it will make more sense for the Reich to work the healthy nail factory crew to death. He passes sentence with a dismissive wave of the hand: "For now, boys, just beat them up real good."

It takes William three weeks to recover from the rifle-butt strikes. The miracle reprieve is no cause for celebration. Berlin has accelerated the extermination schedule and Goeth's killings become totally random. William is outside his barrack one morning talking to a newly arrived prisoner when two SS men collar them both.

> For nothing. They were just combing the camp looking for victims. They took us into an administrative building, marched us up to an attic loft and made us stand in a line with six other guys. Then the psychological torture game began.
>
> One guard said, "The commandant is coming to inspect you. Salute him and tell him your name and work assignment. Address him as 'Herr Commandant' and make it good, because if you don't say it perfectly he'll shoot you. Whatever you do, don't let him see any fear. If he sees you're even just a little bit scared he'll shoot you."

Two minutes later we hear the door slam down-
stairs. Then we hear Goeth walking up the stairs on
my right. He's a big fat guy so you can hear him clomp
on each step. Suddenly there he was with his pistol in
his hand. He looked seven-feet tall with his hat on, all
decked out in black and gray with shiny knee boots.

I was the third guy in line and I raised my hand
up to my head right away so I would be ready to salute.
My hand was shaking and I was trying to think what I
was going to say when he shot the first guy in the head
before he could get a word out.

Now my whole body starts shaking because I know
I'm going to die. He shoots the second guy and walks
past me like I'm invisible. Then he shoots number four,
five, six, and seven and walks downstairs leaving me
and the eighth man standing. He was in the building
two minutes and never said a word.

In front of peers Goeth likes to flaunt his immunity as a
Special Forces operator in a secret program. While drunk at
Oskar Schindler's house he brags that only SS warriors are
cold enough to poke their noses right into the gore. It delights
him when the tractors that terrace his camp scrape open two
old Jewish graveyards. The musty remnants of those dead are
quickly followed by the queer-smelling smoke that seeps down
from the hill.

Plaszow abuts malarial marshland and a woman who
sleeps next to Rosalie develops the telltale chills. When two
more prisoners complain of fever she has to beg the barrack
administrator for permission to tend the ill. She strips a skirt
from a corpse outside and rips it into rags. After long days on

the body wagon at night she soaks rags in water to cool hot brows.

In the middle of her nursing stint she gets the strangest news from a friend who works in the infirmary. Her friend has been helping camp doctors take blood samples from prisoners. These samples are so large and so frequent the prisoners are often unable to walk back to their barracks. At night, her friend now tells her, the doctors pour all the blood down the drain.

After the fight in the nail factory William loses his job outside the camp and is transferred to a sheet metal factory.

"I wasn't there very long and I never understood what was supposed to be happening in this place. My instructor gave me pieces of metal and a hammer and told me to make some noise every once in a while. It was pretend work, but I was grateful for the breather because I still hurt from the beating."

Cut off from the world outside, William must network much harder to ferret up extra bread or the rare slice of meat. When he finds food he sneaks it to his sister and wife. The guards know the inmates are spent at night so they run fewer dog patrols inside the fence after sunset. Slipping outside his barrack, William dodges watchtower searchlights on his way to Rosalie's barrack in the women's camp.

"Thanks to the many chances he took I constantly knew less hunger than those with no such provider," she says. "In spite of all the people we saw shot and hanged for smuggling he kept risking his life to make sure Dorothy and I would survive."

Standing in the dark against her barrack wall the couple can briefly share each other's troubles and a kiss. These late-night rendezvous keep them relatively sane until September 7, 1943. That afternoon William finishes his shift and walks up a sloping road from the camp's industrial section toward his barrack. He is proud of himself, having scored a good-sized piece of bread from a new arrival. He knows Rosalie will be extra pleased when he visits her tonight. As he savors the happy moment one of his wife's friends comes running toward him with a pained face.

"Such a strange look. I said, 'What's wrong?' She said, 'She's gone.' Then she started crying and said, 'They took a bunch of people on a transport to a new camp.' I heard the words 'new camp' and lost my mind. Rose and my sister were all I had left. Now I have bread for my wife but no wife. I went berserk."

He runs to the office of the Jewish police and demands to know the destination of the last transport train. The team he declined to join give him a frosty reception. He barges into the main room in search of chief Willek Chilowicz. Repeatedly told to leave, he refuses. During the commotion an old acquaintance recognizes his voice. Marysia Chilowicz emerges from a back room. When William asks his spurned girlfriend for help he ends up with a laser-eyed harpy in his face.

"She says, 'Now you want to talk to me? Now you need my help? Find the little whore yourself!' I said, 'Marysia, please, have a heart.' She told me to get out or she'd call a guard. I told her to go to hell. She gave me a crazy smile and ran outside. A minute later she came back with a Black Uniform. He dragged me out the door."

William resists the guard and the Ukrainian starts to unsnap his holster. Both fall and wrestle on the dirty campground.

I think I was ready to be killed. Something just came over me. I kept yelling, "Where is my wife? Where is my wife?" Some other prisoners tried to pull us apart and I got hit on the back of the head with a club or a gun. A few hours later I woke up in my barrack with my head split and bleeding. Somebody told me the guards killed two of the prisoners who tried to pull us apart. How I got back to my barrack and why they didn't shoot me I don't know.

For the next three days I went back to work in the factory. I hit the metal pieces with the hammer. Bang, bang, tap, tap. I couldn't sleep at night because I kept worrying about Rose. She was a refined young girl and I didn't think she'd be able to survive without somebody protecting her. All kinds of terrible scenarios were racing through my head. It was killing me. My sister tried to settle me down but it didn't work. Wherever they took Rose, that's where I needed to go.

My brilliant plan was to sneak down to the railway spur by the main gate and climb into a boxcar. This was not a hard thing to do because the Germans didn't guard empty boxcars. We normally spent all our time and energy trying to stay out of them.

The next morning the guards loaded twenty prisoners into the car. The first guys who climbed in looked confused when they saw me crouching in a corner. I put my finger on my lips so they wouldn't say anything. Then the Germans slammed the door and off we all went to Auschwitz. So much for the brilliant plan.

chapter four

"It has to have an end"

One hundred and twenty people can barely breathe, so tightly is the boxcar packed. Down the tracks it lumbers under a quarter moon past farm fields ready for harvest. Some prisoners sleep standing up; one pinned against the wall next to Rosalie looks like he's asleep. His body will be offloaded soon with others gone breathless.

There was screaming when the guards whipped everybody in. Now it's hushed. Blue-black light from a little window high up in a corner paints the prisoners' heads and shoulders. This is the first of four nights without food or water. Prisoners must relieve themselves where they stand.

The wheels clack on the tracks. Sometimes the train stops and stands for hours. Three times soldiers pull off the dead. On the third day there's enough room for the weakest to sit on the squalid floor. Nobody wants to sit but nobody can stand up four days in a row.

Rosalie is right under the window. She tries to distract herself from her burning gut by staring out at the sky. She sees clouds and the odd flight of birds, little black things. When the car stops for hours on the last night she fixes on a speck of

light far away. Suffocating in the stench she watches the star
sparkle. Finally the car shuttles into a yard where the door
jerks open and screaming soldiers beckon with big hands.

"*Raus! Raus! Verfluchte Juden!* Get out, you damned Jews!"

She screams when a German Shepherd lunges at her face.
Women are separated from men and forced through a tall
gate, eyes adjusting to another endless complex of barracks.
One of the girls hears a name and it passes through the ranks.
Skarzysko. For the next year and a half this is home. "Now I
am all alone in the world," Rosalie thinks.

She belongs to Paul Budin, general manager of the defense firm Hugo Schneider AG, also called HASAG. Budin
is a high-ranking Nazi and one of hundreds of soldier-busi-
nessmen getting rich off the war. Originally a manufacturer
of lamps, HASAG now makes bullets and shells for tanks,
underwater mines, and the *Panzerfaust* anti-tank grenade
launcher.

When Budin opened his first factories in conquered Poland the German managers quickly become frustrated with
local Polish workers. The executives eventually opt for Jewish
work slaves under teams of Polish foremen and German supervisors. Responsible for half the Jewish slave deaths in the
General Government, HASAG supports the Nazi concept of
"destruction by work." Twenty thousand human beings per-
ish to maximize Budin's profit margins and personal plun-
der. Women make perfect expendable drones because the SS
charges less for females.

In the isolated village of Skarzysko, workers bunk in the
same stark barracks Rosalie knew at Plaszow. She gets the
same diet of tasteless bread and soup, and for the first week
the same work assignment. Making rounds through the camp

with a wagon, she fills three giant barrel-like receptacles with the corpses she gathers.

HASAG spends no money to keep worker housing clean and Skarzysko teems with lice. The first day Rosalie walks into her barrack she sees waves of the tiny bloodsuckers rippling on the walls and mattresses.

"Sleep was our one chance to forget our troubles, but every time you were about to doze off you felt a bite. Everybody was always scratching and the bites would get infected and crusty and ooze. After a month or two you thought you were going to lose your mind. A lot of people threw themselves on the electrified fence just because of the lice."

After a month she is assigned to Plant A, one of three main munitions factories. With winter approaching, a roof overhead sounds like a blessing and she hopes for the best as she reports for duty. The female German work crew supervisor grew up in Poland. Pavlovska is a tall, broad-hipped brunette in her late twenties. She wears her hair pulled back, no make-up and a black and white enamel swastika pin on her dark civilian skirt and jacket uniform.

We were standing in line in this big dirty factory full of noisy metalworking machinery. I was minding my own business, looking down at my feet. Suddenly I was also looking down at a pair of great big shiny black shoes. In front of everybody Pavlovska started picking on me. "O, look at the beautiful Jew!" she said. "Are you ready to make bullets for German soldiers, Miss Beautiful Jew? Does that make you happy?"

When I said yes she punched me in the stomach so hard I couldn't breathe. And that was my life for the next eighteen months. *Every day she would say, "Good morning, Miss Beautiful Jew!" Then she punched me or kicked my shins. Always a fist in the back, in the stomach, my shoulders.*

Pretty soon I was covered with bruises. Some of the other girls thought Pavlovska looked Jewish and maybe she got teased for that when she was growing up. Maybe she grew up poor or maybe she hated having such a big butt. Who knows? Whatever her motivations, she was the cruelest, most vicious woman I ever met.

Her husband also worked at Skarzysko as a guard. He had blond hair and blue eyes and a deep voice. Sometimes when she had us assembled he would come over and they would mock us together. More than once I heard her say "the beautiful Jew" to him—die shöne Jude. He would look directly at me and laugh. It made me so uneasy. All I could do was look off to the side.

An experienced slave briefs Rosalie on her job—filling metal canisters with ball bearings. These will become flesh-shredding shrapnel when German tanks fire the shells at Allied soldiers. Nobody can give her a straight answer on the right number of bearings to put in each canister. Different supervisors take turns berating and beating her for adding either too many or too few steel balls.

"It made us sad to think we were helping the Germans fight their battles. The shrapnel I put in these shells may have killed many Russian, British, and American soldiers. In other parts of the plant girls had to make rifle and pistol bullets that were used against our own loved ones closer to home."

Fela is the Jewish prisoner who serves as shift boss in

Plant A. She despises the workers, bows to the Germans, and sleeps with her Polish superior. For sex she gets privileges and a whip.

"They gave her extra bread so she hit us. 'Work,' she was always yelling, 'work, you lazy whores!' It was ironic to be called a whore fifty times a day by the loosest woman in the camp."

A pair of senior Polish supervisors take an interest in Rosalie. The taller man she remembers for his black hair and shiny black eyes. The other is an almost albino blond who loiters behind his fast-talking friend's shoulder and never says a word. They give her extra food and promise to help her escape if she will let them sneak her off the premises.

"They acted so nice it didn't feel right. They gave me fruit, even chocolate sometimes, always asking me to run away with them to freedom. Maybe they were great humanitarians. I always said no."

No one has any time alone. Shuttling to and fro in her work gang or wedged between bunkmates, she ends up craving solitude. It can be found only at night and only in the rankest space of all. The camp latrine is long boards with a dozen holes over an open trench. The slimy floor is alive with roaches. But for as long as a prisoner can block out the smell she is free to be her own person. One night Rosalie finds a broom leaning against the wall and starts to dance with it.

> *Don't ask me why. I was young and probably just bored. But I got carried away and started humming the tango song they played the night I met William. One of the regular army soldiers outside heard me and came in when I wasn't looking. This was a fat old man*

we called The Pipe because he was always puffing on one. He had chased me with a stick once before, but we didn't take him seriously because we never saw him kill anybody. When The Pipe saw me dancing he got really mad. A Jew dancing in his prison?

"Ach!" he shouts, "verfluchte Jude! O, you damned Jew!"

He grabbed the broom and gave me a good crack over the head with it. It hurt a lot but an SS man would have shot me.

On the worst days there are selections. *Sortierung* is the German word. It means "to sort things out" or "to separate one grade of merchandise from another." All the prisoners must strip for the camp doctors. Those judged too feeble for work get sorted into trucks, driven to a field called Sczelnice, and shot by the factory police. So everyone pinches her cheeks and does what little else she can to prolong an illusion of vitality.

Labor and hunger have drained Rosalie's body. Never heavy to begin with, she dwindled during the famine in the ghetto. After more privation at Plaszow her system has begun to eat its own muscle. She stops menstruating, her joints ache, and her ankles swell. Her heart skips beats and surges and she gets dizzy standing during the evening count. Two nights ago she almost blacked out. And it's turned cold again. As the weather worsens the guards make the slaves stand outside for hours in the wooden clog shoes that fill easily with slush. She has no stockings, but she does have the brown jacket William gave her back at Plaszow a few days before they were separated.

On top of the physical stress there are emotional blows.

Last week a good friend died in her sleep. The week before that, an even closer friend grabbed the fence and rode the voltage into the next dimension.

> *Just when you thought you had a grip on your sanity something would knock you off balance again. A girl in my barrack was five months pregnant from her husband. Goeth murdered him back in Plaszow. When she started to show we made a cloth bandage out of a sheet and she wrapped her belly tight so the Germans couldn't notice.*
>
> *It worked for a while but one night she woke up in labor. When the baby was born some of the girls strangled it and threw it in the latrine. They felt they had to do it because if the guards found out they would kill the baby and the mother, too. This way only the baby was gone. When I heard about this my spirits plunged. An innocent little thing, right into the toilet. But you couldn't give up on yourself. There were always other people who needed help.*

In the middle of November, Goeth sends Budin an extra 2,000 slaves. After a shift in the factory Rosalie is getting in line for her soup ration when she hears a familiar voice.

> *I saw Mania, my sister's best friend who lived above us on Dietlovska Street. She was the sweetest girl in the world but helpless. I went over and hugged her and we both cried about our families.*
>
> *I warned her that this was a place where you either got tough or you gave up. When I first got there I cried*

around the clock because I lost a lot of hope when I lost
William. But an older woman set me straight. She said,
"You won't make it here if you don't try a lot harder."
So I got focused.

And it helped that I had a little tomboy in me to
start with. But Mania never played kickball or went
sledding when we were young. She was always a tiny
delicate girl who liked to do embroidery. And she had
wasted away to nothing. She had great big black eyes
and looked like a baby bird with no feathers.

I made sure she stood next to me during every selec-
tion and made her stand on her tiptoes to look as tall
as possible. During one really tough selection I had her
stand on two rocks. The factory police got a lot of girls
that day but the rocks worked for Mania, thank God.

At Skarzysko the saddest spectacle are the workers in Plant
C, the Reich's biggest dynamite factory. The boxy old foundry
is draped with camo netting to fool Allied bombers. Day after
day, trains packed with crates of the explosive sticks head east
from Plant C to the Russian front. Inside the unventilated brick
cavern, sweat-drenched crews pour powder into molds, rig the
fuses, and cook the sticks in banks of furnaces. The air is full
of burning dust and sulfur toxins that invade the slaves' bodies
twelve hours a day until their flesh turns bright yellow.

"We called them 'canaries.' Even the most selfish prisoners
tossed them little pieces of bread when they passed us on their
way to work. Everybody in the camp had sunken cheeks, but
when you looked at the canaries all you saw was eyes and skull."

Every work day is indistinguishable from the next. Without newspapers or calendars the women can't track the sea-

sons. One morning the girls can clearly sense the winter of the second year ending. A warm golden light spreads on the barrack roof as the guards call roll.

I did my best to look after Mania and tried not to get killed myself. The only way I kept it together was with a little mantra. A thousand times a day I'd say it over and over. "This had a beginning, so it has to have an end. This had a beginning, so it has to have an end." It was an immature way of coping with the situation, but I had to have something and that was all I had.

I also started smoking. I had seen other girls pick up cigarette butts off the floor and thought I would never touch the filthy things. The first time I did it I couldn't believe it. My father would have been so ashamed. After a while I would pick one up as soon as a guard cast it aside. Anything to calm my nerves.

The two Polish supervisors kept pushing me to sneak out into the countryside with them. The black-haired man was very persistent. He said, "You don't even look Jewish. We can smuggle you to Slovakia. You don't need to be a victim of this program." This made me so angry. I never really trusted these guys so I told them, "You know what? This program killed my father, my mother and my whole family. Let it kill me, too."

This is why I never took a bath for two and a half years. When you were naked you were vulnerable and some girls found that out the hard way in the showers. Better to be dirty than sorry was my philosophy. I knew I could always take a bath after the war if I made it all the way through.

chapter five

"I wish I could have helped more people"

Outside the front gate at Auschwitz a dead man is bound to a post with ropes around his chest, thighs, and throat. He wears dull gray pajamas with fat navy stripes. Over his heart an upside-down yellow triangle points to a hole in his pajama top that matches the hole in his back. From these holes, a gallon of dark stain has drained into the uniform. While rows of bald prisoners file past the dead man a live orchestra on a bandstand plays an upbeat march. It's a sparkling fall day.

When Heinrich Himmler toured the camp the year before, commandant Rudolph Hess confided that he was having trouble with escapes. The SS National Leader told Hess to prop up every escapee his men shot as a display at the main gate. He felt that terror was the only language prisoners from more than twenty countries could all understand.

When Himmler had taken charge of the SS in 1929 it was a street gang with 200 members. He now commands 800,000 men and the new army that grew out of the Death Head assassination teams. He runs thousands of secret prison camps, major industrial companies, a military spy network and the Gestapo political police. As Germany's master of "inferior races" throughout the conquered lands he has authority to work slaves to death and to exterminate millions of non-workers. He chose Auschwitz as his main killing site because it has fabulous railroad access. The site will devour 1,200,000 Jews and half a million other prisoners. Some days, 20,000 people die in the gas chambers. During his visit, Himmler watched through a peephole while a trainload of Dutch Jews were put down.

He believes in Hitler so fiercely regular army generals call him the Fuhrer's dog. At Auschwitz, Himmler's cult of blind obedience clones men like Josef Mengele, who jumps up and down in fury when a nurse refuses to kill a baby. "*Befehl ist befehl!*" Mengele screams. An order is an order.

William stumbles into this regimented system in September 1943. As far as the schedulers at the German railway company are concerned there are only twenty "special passengers" in his boxcar, not twenty-one. The transportation authority charges the government a standard bulk freight rate to carry the men down the line. When the car stops at the Krakow station William can hear workers joking and laughing outside the car. A paycheck is all it takes for them to sign off on genocide.

The trip from Krakow to the old Polish town of Oswiecim takes a few hours. Thousands have been shipped in these cars before and the wooden floorboards are sticky and slick. When the door finally jerks open William jumps down into gummy ankle-deep mud and a crowd of barking guards. Seven thousand Death Head soldiers work at Auschwitz and half of them seem to be on duty the day William runs the gauntlet of hard eyes and skull badges.

The guards beat us through the fence into a compound and made us strip in a shower facility. My first impression was how clean everything was compared to Goeth's camp.

I was standing there naked with an envelope folded up in my hand. There were three little photos in it—one of Rose, one of my mom, one of my sister Dorothy. A guard told me to give it to him. I hesitated for half a second and he punched me in the mouth and took it away. I could taste blood and I cried because it hurt and because it felt like these people were being taken away from me all over again.

We got our tattoos in another room from prisoners sitting behind tables. The guards made us sit down and a little guy dipped his needle in ink and branded me like an animal. Number 174248. The barbers shaved our heads and bodies and we had our pictures taken and went into the showers where they made us get into tubs of strong-smelling chemicals. This dip killed lice. We ended up in a big cold room with a cement floor where they threw us our pajamas and wooden clogs.

Cloth badges on every prisoner's jacket and right pant leg help the guards figure out how much violence to dish out. Common criminals who can pretend to be of Aryan ancestry get a green badge and generally suffer the least abuse. Under new Nazi laws they can languish in prison forever for petty offenses like shoplifting, but they will not be systematically tortured. "Anti-social" men who may have been alcoholics or chronic troublemakers get brown badges and are shown no respect. Jehovah's Witnesses wear purple patches for refusing to swear loyalty to Hitler. Homosexuals wear pink because Himmler thinks their lifestyle endangers German society.

William gets the yellow Jew badge that marks him as an eminently expendable creature, a punching bag at every guard's disposal. Another prisoner tells him they are considered political prisoners because Hitler has spun his recent invasion of Russia as a crusade against "Judeo-Bolshevism." Nazi media outlets are busy portraying Judaism as the bedrock of modern communism, a system William despises.

There's the insanity of the whole thing. If I had any politics at that age I was anti-Communist. That's why I refused to let my family go to Russia. Marxism was the stupidest concept on earth and most of the people I knew felt the same way. But the Nazis said every Jew was a Marxist terrorist. These politicians demonized us with words and make-believe associations so they could steal our homes and businesses.

I was standing there and I heard a voice say, "There's a Schiff!" I looked around and saw Nathan, the son of my father's old business partner. He and a rough-looking Polish prisoner were helping the Germans process the new guys. They walked up to me and Nathan said, "Which of the guys who came in on your train have gold?"

Obviously they wanted to rob somebody and one guy on the train did tell me he was smuggling gold. Men who did this had to hide it in their rectums. The guy in the boxcar was a total stranger to me, but I liked him. Nathan I never liked. When we were kids we both used to sweep up hair in the first barber shop our fathers owned together. He was always pushy.

When I met him at Auschwitz he said, "You have no idea what it's like here and you won't make it without friends. If you help us we'll make sure you get bread." I played dumb and they left me alone.

The guards took us to Block 1. This was the temporary housing block run by a German criminal. The SS shipped this guy out of a prison in their country where he was doing hard time and brought him to Poland to supervise foreign prisoners. He had a green badge and a wooden club like a baseball bat. He said we'd be in quarantine with him while he showed us the ropes.

The training block was made of bricks. There was a cellar and an upstairs level, sinks with hot water, and an indoor toilet. The German had a private room by the main door and he assigned me my own bunk with a mattress and a clean blanket. There was not a speck of dirt or dust anywhere. Again, compared to Plaszow, the place seemed like a hotel. It was so nice nobody knew what to think.

Symmetry, cleanliness, and order are in overdrive everywhere. The Polish prisoners marvel at the perfectly level paved roads outside the block. Inside, their new master is obsessed with punctilious bedmaking. Every tuck and crease must be precise. Everywhere signs warn: "Lice kill!" The discovery of a single bug can send all the men back through the disinfectant dip. William is intrigued by the camp's "dry" form of lice control, huge machines that bombard the hairless men with radio waves.

*The guards woke us up with shouting very early every
morning. Prisoners would go outside for roll call and
we were counted over and over to make sure nobody
had escaped. We'd get a slice of bread and a cup of
dark water they called coffee. The German taught us
to wash our cups and put them back in the pantry by
the front door.*

*It was like this for four days. If I wasn't so torn up
over losing Rose it would have almost been restful. On
the fifth morning we were standing outside and they
called my number. It's hard for your brain to get used to
the fact that it's really you they want when they shout
out "Seven-seven-four-two-four-eight!"*

*They called some more numbers and we formed
lines five across and marched to Block 4. This was
our permanent assignment. Our new boss was inside,
another German gangster with a barrel chest and the
same kind of wooden bat. Right away he clubbed a
skinny old guy unconscious and said, "That's how it
works around here when I'm in a good mood."*

One hundred prisoners live in Block 4. The occupancy
limit is enforced by selections every morning. For every hardy
new arrival a worn-out worker must go.

*A guy told me there was another camp close by where
they burned people in ovens. That's where the smoke
came from that stank up the whole countryside. The
abundance of this smoke scared me to death. At Plaszow
you knew your odds weren't good, but at Auschwitz they
sorted out so many people you had no chance at all.*

The gangster could only keep a hundred men but new trains came in every day and new faces kept showing up at the door. So if he didn't like you or you got too skinny you went to the ovens or he beat you to death.

After you saw him beat a few people to death you got smart. Smart people avoided attention at all cost. One day a new prisoner took my bunk. He wasn't a Jew and he knew that I couldn't afford to make a scene. So I slept on the floor and kept trying to figure out how I could make the gangster like me.

He had his own table where he ate his meals just outside his private bedroom at the far end of the barrack. When he ate he could watch everybody and we could all see him. He had three personal assistants who sat with him: a tailor who made his uniforms, his barber, and his cook. A couple times I heard him yell at his cook about how bad the food was.

But he protected these three guys from the ovens. They got to stay inside while everybody else went out in the morning to get sorted. From the minute I heard the word "ovens" my top priority was to get a chair at the gangster's table. And I knew I didn't have a lot of time because I was starting to get skinny.

At roll call one morning the new men get their first duty assignments. William and four others are pulled out of the ranks to join a waiting column of fifteen. As they march through the main gate he gets an eyeful of big black iron letters against the sky.

"You know the famous sign in all the old pictures. 'Work is freedom.' I read that and then I looked over and saw a dead prisoner tied to a post with a crow sitting on his head. This guy tried to run away from his work so naturally I was curious what kind of job they had waiting for me."

The prisoners proceed south to the small village of Raisko and the Waffen SS Hygiene Institute where different medical corps departments study serums, bacteria, and war chemistry. Chief physicians Munch and Weber work their staffs overtime in search of new immunization compounds to protect German troops from disease. By some accounts an ethical doctor, Munch will later admit to participating in experiments in the same block where most of Josef Mengele's atrocities took place. The first thing William notices is that the Hygiene Institute has no windows.

> They led us to a super-clean room and told us to sit in a row of chairs against the wall. After half an hour a doctor wearing glasses and a white coat came in with an assistant to take our temperature and heart rate. This doctor was a prisoner, too, but a calm and distinguished man. You could tell by looking at him that he was extremely intelligent.
>
> He treated me very respectfully, the first time any camp official had done so. He introduced himself as Dr. Meisel from Lvov and asked me if I was Jewish. He said he was Jewish, too, and said I reminded him of his own children. He told me how he had been taken prisoner and assigned to his job to create serums that could some day help a lot of people.
>
> Then he gave everybody a shot. Every syringe had a number on it. When he gave me my injection I could tell he hated what he was doing. My arm started to

burn and a few other guys started cramping and throwing up. Dr. Meisel told us to go lie down in the next room. Every hour he and the assistant came back to check on us and make notes on a clipboard. Two prisoners passed out and were removed from the room by assistants. I never saw them again so I assume they died. The last time Dr. Meisel checked my pulse he told me in a low voice that he'd do what he could to help me.

We marched back to Block 4 and the next morning one of the guys who took a shot was too sick to get out of his bunk. The rest of us marched back to Raisko and lined up in the same room for another round of shots. When Dr. Meisel came out he told the guard that his assistant was sick and he wanted me as a replacement. I was very, very lucky to get out of the shot line. The Russian kid who was sitting in the chair next to me got my shot and died half an hour later from violent seizures. A boy not older than sixteen.

For the rest of the day I followed Dr. Meisel around doing whatever he told me to do. "William, please hand me syringe number seven. William, take the empty syringes to the lab." Nothing very complicated. That afternoon before we were marched back he took me aside and said, "Here we do what we have to do so we can do a little good when we have the chance." Basically, the Germans told him he could be a doctor or go to the ovens. He was doing what he could to stay human and he definitely saved my life that day.

The hospital job keeps William warm while men on construction, road, and farm crews falter in the snow. As his friendship with the doctor deepens the older man begins to speak of his young unmarried daughter back in Lvov. He knows that William's wife, trapped in one of the scattered camps, will probably not survive. He also knows that after the war most Jewish men will be dead and his daughter's bridal options constricted.

William is treated well by other staffers. He wears laundered white overalls and gets a chance to practice his German with educated prisoners from Strasbourg and Vienna. For a while he acts as a lookout for two Jewish doctors having an affair, a German man in his late forties and a much younger Frenchwoman. He mops the hall in front of the bathroom the lovers use for their liaisons and rattles the mop bucket as a warning whenever guards encroach.

Every night he returns to Block 4 and an overlord who uses prisoners as human footstools during bunk checks. In his third month he starts to see men sorted out for the ovens who look arguably healthier than he does. One morning the guards make the prisoners stand in the rain for three hours and William picks up the kind of sore throat that can get a man turned into smoke. He keeps losing weight and his chest muscles have all but melted away. Nobody is getting their allotted calories because kitchen workers and deliverymen steal the prisoners' meat and vegetables. The smuggler who kept nine people alive in the ghetto knows he must organize with a vengeance to save himself. But the easy opportunities have already been covered and prisoners are competing like mad for flunky jobs in the SS barracks where food scraps are rumored to be plentiful.

Late one overcast afternoon William walks past the motor pool adjacent to the Hygiene Institute. Watching the mechanics fiddle with a motorcycle reminds him of happier days in the bike shop back in Krakow. Then a truck pulls up and the driver and his helper start unloading their goods. From a safe distance, as inconspicuously as possible, William sees the two men carry six sides of beef into a meat locker in the garage bay. In the camp's underground economy, a stolen pound of margarine is worth sixty dollars and a pound of meat is worth $250. A thousand pounds of high-value animal protein turbocharge the imagination.

> *This meat was for SS guards and officers. They stored it near the lab so our technicians could check it for poison before it went to the kitchen. I knew right away that if I could get a job in the garage I'd have a chance to make it through the war. Dr. Meisel recommended me to the garage administrator and this man asked me what I knew about cars. I said I knew everything, hoping my experience with bikes would help me bluff my way through until I caught on.*
>
> *On Dr. Meisel's recommendation they put me in charge of the two real mechanics, a Russian teenager and a Czech who was older than me. These guys didn't speak any German but I was getting pretty good at it and could translate work orders into something the Slavic guys understood. Usually all we did were oil changes and basic truck maintenance so everything worked out okay.*
>
> *When I was sure this job was stable I went and knocked on the big gangster's bedroom door. He gave me a hard look. I took my cap off and said, "Excuse me, Herr Room Senior. I hope you don't mind, but I think I have a way to provide you with real meat on a regular*

basis." I was taking a big chance. He could have killed me right then just for making the offer. But every day at Auschwitz was already a big chance and I knew he could protect me from the selections.

He told me to come into his room and we sat at his table. He wanted to know how I could get access to such a precious commodity. He thought it would be impossible for me to hide the meat on my body and get it back into the camp past the gate guards. This was the guy I'd been hiding from ever since I showed up. Now we were face to face and he was starting to sound angry. He had scars on his face and knuckles from fighting and his nose looked like it had been broken more than once.

I told him I was one of the best smugglers in Krakow and explained the chicken-belt system my mother designed. I said I thought his tailor could make me a pair of tight underpants with a pocket on the bottom between the legs. This idea sold him. The tailor measured me and made a perfect garment out of a sheet that night. When I was leaving for work the next morning the Room Senior grabbed my elbow. He said, "It's a good plan, but you better not get caught."

That afternoon I snuck into the locker and used a screwdriver to hack off a flap of meat, almost a pound. I smuggled it back and the gangster had his cook fry it in his bedroom and let me eat some with him. I don't know how long he was in prison before Auschwitz, but the way he wolfed this food down I don't think he'd seen a steak in years. When he was done he said, "Okay, Jew, what do you want?"

When I told him he walked me out into the block and over to the guy who took my bunk. He ordered him to find another place to sleep and he told everybody this was now my bunk permanently. The next morning he walked me over to the soldier who was in charge of the roll call. He said, "This is my Jew and I need him for chores in the block. Can we excuse him from the counts?" The soldier said, sure, no problem.

And that was it. For thirteen months I stole meat from the locker and fed this murderer. Once he needed me my life changed. Getting exempted from selections is the main reason I survived Auschwitz. The guards spot-checked me many times when I was smuggling but I never got caught. That didn't mean it was easy. Your heart was always in your throat.

Now that bread wasn't a problem for me I was able to help a few people with food. One night a bunch of men by the fence were talking to some women on the other side who had come in from Plaszow that afternoon. Through the fence I saw my aunt, my mom's youngest sister Pola. For two or three weeks I did what I could for her, passing her food and tissue paper through the fence. Then she disappeared.

Sometimes I have dreams about women begging for bread on the other side of a fence. I wish I could have helped more people.

William leaves the garage one afternoon and enters the Hygiene Institute to sneak in a quick visit with Dr. Meisel. He can't find his protector in the deserted halls or laboratories and assumes the entire staff has been called up to the main camp. He hears an abrupt high-pitched scream.

> *Wild screaming, horrible, coming from an operating room a little further up the hallway. The door was cracked and I looked in. Two doctors were cutting on a Russian girl with a saw, taking off her forearm with no anesthesia. They already had her hand off. It was on a tray.*
>
> *The girl was tied to the table and struggled until she fainted. She may have been twelve years old and her blood was all over their smocks and the table. As soon as they sawed the forearm off they threw it on the floor and started to stitch the hand to the stump of her elbow. I went outside and threw up.*
>
> *That afternoon I hacked meat off a side of beef and smuggled it back to the block as usual. I wish I could say I had no appetite but after five years of being treated worse than animals we stayed pretty focused on soup and bread, soup and bread. Survival was our obsession. It's an awful, awful feeling.*
>
> *In my bunk that night I remembered how I had thought my father was an ignorant person for worrying about the Germans. I always assumed that the smarter a civilization is, the nobler it has to be. I finally realized that smart men can be the cruelest and most deceptive.*

For fifteen months this black hole is William's home. Every day the bell wakes the men and the work details form their ranks of five. Every day the orchestra plays a sprightly march from a short song list that never changes. Prisoners doff their caps to salute the duty officers and pass under the black letters of the gate.

The crew en route to Raisko walk along the Sola River as the sun pops up over the hills. They watch the train from Krakow to Berlin fly by, full of German citizens who have a lot to worry about now that the war isn't going well. More strange smoke blows over from the distant chimneys, another trainload of Hungarian Jews.

William helps the Czech mechanic straighten out the handlebars on a motorcycle an SS sergeant laid down on a road outside the camp. The sergeant blamed the bad Polish roads but the two prisoners suspect the potent local schnapps. They stop the grease monkey banter when they hear a buzzing overhead. They gaze up into the bright August blue, hands shielding eyes, but can't find the silhouette.

At 10:30 the next morning there's a more intense drone overhead when the sergeant comes by to pick up his bike. He rides off in a hurry as soon as flak barrages start breaking in the clouds. Gun stations in Krakow and Katowice are trying to knock down the Fifth Bomb Wing of the US Fifteenth Air Force.

The Flying Fortresses pass through relatively unmolested and dump 300 tons of bombs on the I.G. Farben synthetic oil plant just a few miles east of the main camp. William and the Czech mechanic stand and listen to the explosions. The Hygiene Institute doctors come running outside. They cock their heads and squint and try to make sense of the noise.

In Block 4 that night the prisoners debate the significance of the raid. One says he hopes the Allies will return and bomb every inch of the camp. It will mean death, he admits, but a fast clean death and justice.

William is tinkering under a truck hood when the flak guns start pounding three weeks later. Once again, American bomber command ignores the gas chambers and ovens. All ninety-six planes have been sent to pulverize the oil plant. Three B-24 Liberators fall in flames from the sky. The rest drop their loads and never return.

Nothing seems to change in the enormous secret prison. Goeth sends another 2,000 Jews down for burning. Fifteen-year-old Anne Frank has her head shaved and a number inked into her arm. Fourteen-hundred boys from the children's block turn to smoke. In Block 11, the political officers pop holes in heads with small quiet pistols and fry prisoners' faces on the stove. During the week of Yom Kippur, Dr. Mengele nails a board to a post so another thousand boys can parade beneath it to see who is tall enough to live.

The following week there's a mutiny by a team of oven workers who suspect they have been slated for extermination. They attack heavily armed guards with shovels, fling an SS trooper into a blazing oven, and blow up the chimney of Crematorium 4. The guards regroup and overcome the rebels with dogs, machine guns, and hand grenades.

Chanukah is celebrated quietly. At Christmas a little tree adorns the gallows. William sits in the Room Senior's bedroom while the cook fries precious purloined meat and the tailor and barber wait for their scraps. The gangster has never been much of a talker but one of the guards has just given him a remarkable scoop.

"Hitler is going to be in New York soon," he says, cocking an eyebrow at his messmates. He lets the news sink in, munching his steak and nodding with stolid pride.

"The Fuhrer has a new weapon. He's taking the battle right to Roosevelt's door."

Stretched in his bunk that night William is depressed.

"I thought, well, it's all over now. The madman is going to take over the whole world. That's the kind of information vacuum we lived in. Sometimes we got bits of the truth from new prisoners. They would tell us that Hitler lost Paris or that the Russians were picking up steam. But basically we were in the dark. So I believed the Block Elder. And I was crushed. We were all counting on America. It was our ace in the hole."

chapter six

"Remember how I lived my life, Rose"

It's four in the morning at Camp Skarzysko. Rosalie sleeps with two other women on a bottom bunk shelf. During the winter of 1944 shared body warmth has been a lifesaver in the drafty barrack. Mania sleeps on one side of Rosalie and their friend sleeps on the other. Lately a bad case of dysentery has kept this girl running to the latrine.

At four in the morning Rosalie wakes up and senses something real wrong. Both she and the sick girl sleep on their right sides and as usual she can feel knees against the back of her thighs. But the body behind her isn't making breathing noises. Not wanting to acknowledge this, she does nothing. There's no point in rushing the inevitable. The two hours will fly by before they must carry their friend out and set her in the dirt by the door where strangers will strip off her clothes. In the bunk for those two hours at least the dead woman will retain a little dignity.

When the wake-up bell sounds Rosalie helps move the body through the door while Mania falls to pieces. She tries not to look at the gaping mouth and unblinking eyes. During months of loading her body cart she has seen hundreds of these faces. This face belonged to a friend. Setting the body down by the door, she decides to stop making friends. From here on out it's just her and Mania. That's all the heart she has left.

Lots of girls have dysentery now and the latrine stinks worse than ever. The summer heat explodes the smell. Rosalie staggers out gasping one morning and finds her normal space in the roll call yard. Something different is happening today, something bad. There are many more guards swaggering around than usual. There's The Pipe, the blustery fool who hit her with the broom. He has his helmet cinched up tight under his many chins, trying to act tough. The last time Rosalie saw her captors massing like this was at Plaszow, the day they whipped so many slaves onto the train.

Sure enough, as soon as the whole barrack assembles an officer commands the women to form fives. Before the prisoners can react, the guards start pushing and prodding. Out the gate they hustle the women past the factories. Ripples of panic run through the ranks and Rosalie starts the mantra. "This had a beginning, so it has to have an end. This had a beginning ...."

Incantation doesn't defuse the stress. This unexplained change may prove the mantra true. Today may really be the end. Rumors about death camps have gone around. She and Mania wonder what the monsters have in mind until the railway station comes into view. The soldiers cram people into the cars and slam the door. The engine lurches, the couplings rattle and the wheels start clacking on the tracks.

Two days, two nights. No water or food. On the last night Rosalie coughs, usually not a big deal. But a catching second cough throws a thick salty fluid over her tongue. She spits this into her palm. In the weak dawn leaking through the little window the spit looks black. Internal bleeding, a disheartening milestone.

After an eternity in limbo the doors fly open and the drill begins with the standard harangue. Out, damned Jews, stinking Jews, filthy Jews. More big dogs, more fists cracking whips outside another barbed wire fort. The women blink in the sun while a new name circulates. It sounds like CHOM-sta-ho.

"Today I can't visualize the surroundings of this last camp very well. Once we went in I didn't look outside very much. I had a funny feeling I might never leave. Inside it was the exact same thing—slaves making killing tools until it was their turn to be shot. Another day in Hitlerland."

In August 1944, Paul Budin has moved 5,000 HASAG slaves west, out of the path of Russia's dynamic summer offensive. The barracks at his main bullet factory in the Polish town of Czestochowa are jammed to the rafters with new arrivals. Many will die of starvation, typhus, and the sadism of the SS guards who will soon take over.

> We were so skinny and hungry and demolished we started to believe it didn't make any difference if we lived or died. The weaker we got, the more abuse they gave us. That winter the guards would make you stand outside all day barefoot in buckets of ice water. And every survivor of this filthy camp remembers how intense the lice were. Much worse even than Skarzysko. They burrowed under my skin faster than I could dig them out.
>
> After we settled into the routine we got a morning bread ration and somebody said, "Today is Yom Kippur." I lost a lot of faith in God when I saw the

slaughter at the orphanage, but I also came from a very
observant family and Yom Kippur is Yom Kippur. So I
decided to fast. I was hoping that if I didn't eat, maybe
there would be a miracle. Help would come from above
and this hell would suddenly disappear.

I didn't want anybody to steal my piece of bread so
I tucked it inside my blouse. By the time the fast ended
at sundown I thought I might as well save it a little
longer. That way I'd have a big feast for breakfast, two
whole pieces of bread.

When I pulled it out the next morning the lice on
my precious treasure looked like cake frosting. I brushed
them off as best I could and ate it anyway. A few little
bugs weren't going to hurt me as much as Pavlovska
and her husband. Both of them got transferred to this
camp with our crew.

Rosalie's supervisor is more vindictive than ever when the
workers are assigned duties at the new factory The leg kicks
keep targeting the same black and bloody sweet spots on her
shins. Punches to the back focus on the kidneys and lungs so
much she wonders if these cause the blood she now spits up
abundantly. One day at noon Pavlovska takes her lunch break
and Rosalie runs to the latrine to rinse lice off her skin.

They were biting my neck, my legs, everywhere. It was
driving me insane. I was gone six minutes and thought
I wouldn't be missed. When I got back she was waiting
for me with her husband and another guard. Finally
I had given Pavlovska an excuse to use as much vio-
lence as she wanted and both men had whips. She said,

"Where did you go, Miss Beautiful Jew? Do you think the rules don't apply to you?"

They stripped me naked in front of everybody. Then they threw me up on a work table and whipped me until I blacked out. I had a lot of boils on my back from malnourishment and the whip tore all these open. I was a bloody mess. My friends picked me up and took me back to my barrack and cleaned me up. I thought I would never, ever have the guts to get up and go to work the next day. But if I didn't get up, they'd kill me.

Two more times she had me whipped for nothing, the last time almost to death. Hate turned her into a demon. At this point in the war the guards were beginning to sense defeat and they focused all their new anger and fear and frustration on us.

Coming back from the latrine one night she rounds the corner of a barrack. There is no moon but a cluster of flames on the ground catches her eye, a small fire built close to a barrack wall. Beside it four women kneel over a body stretched out face down in the snow.

One of them had a sharp piece of metal she must have smuggled out of the factory. She used this to cut meat off the dead girl's bottom. I saw her hand the pieces of meat to the others and they put it on twigs and cooked it over the fire. It was so primitive to see these women crouching down and eating in the dark. I knew one of them pretty well. She always seemed like a nice person.

The strangest thing was the silence. Nobody said a word. I stood there watching them from around the

corner and thought to myself, well, it can't get worse
than this. I was wrong.

A few weeks later she walks past a fence by the men's barracks. One of the men on the other side calls her by name,
a childhood friend from Krakow who has just arrived from
another camp. The two cry as they reminisce.

> *His name was Jonathan and his mother was one of*
> *my mom's best friends. He and his brother played kick-*
> *ball in the park with me and my sister Lucy. These*
> *were the two boys who taught me the game of flicking*
> *stones in the hole. We played it together hundreds of*
> *times. He laughed when I reminded him that I got*
> *good enough to beat them both a few times. It was so*
> *wonderful to see him. He said, "Come by here tomor-*
> *row. A friend of mine has bread and I think I can get*
> *you a piece."*
>
> *That was great news because I was getting weaker*
> *and starting to spit blood every day. I went to bed hap-*
> *py that night. When I came back the next day he looked*
> *around to make sure nobody was watching. Then he*
> *tossed a huge piece of bread and half a carrot over the*
> *fence. I picked these up out of the snow. I said, "Thank*
> *you, Jonathan! Thank you!"*
>
> *We didn't know an SS man had heard us talking*
> *the day before. He was waiting behind a barrack with*
> *some guards. They grabbed Jonathan and hanged him*
> *at roll call the next morning. For my punishment they*
> *made me stand alone in front of the gallows all day. I*
> *had a nervous breakdown and started to pray that one*

of the guards would shoot me. Then I got very sick with
dysentery.

Now it's Rosalie who sleeps on the edge of the bunk shelf
so she can run back and forth to the latrine all night. She
and Mania consider themselves lucky when they get a shelf.
With everybody weakening, fewer people can climb up onto
the upper bunk level and there is competition for the bottom
bed shelf.

The daily bowl of soup can no longer be taken for granted,
either. The kitchen can't keep up with the overcrowding and
some of the men who dispense the slop give their girlfriends
extra ladlefuls as payback for affection. If you do not barter
your body or push, you end up last in line.

> *There was a big frenzy one night and the soup was all*
> *gone when my turn came. The next night someone stole*
> *my bowl. I had to cup my hands and get my dinner that*
> *way. People did this in an emergency. Most of the soup*
> *seeped through my fingers into the dirt.*
>
> *When I cried and started to lick my palms, Mania*
> *offered me some of her soup. Now it was her turn to be*
> *the mother. She kept saying, "Be strong!" But she could*
> *tell there was no more fight in me.*

Mania is not the only one who can sense this vulnerability.
Walking back to the barrack from a night shift at the factory,
Rosalie is tackled from behind and pinned to the ground.

> *If I had screamed the Germans up in the watchtowers*
> *would have machine-gunned me and the idiot who was*

tearing off my underpants. He grabbed my throat and tried to pin me on my back while he got ready to rape me but I kicked him with my heel and hurt him. Fear gave me the strength. He got up and ran away and I went inside the barrack. I was shaking and crying with my neck bleeding from his fingernails.

You want to know how sick and upside down our lives were? What scared me most, more than the shame I would have felt if he had violated me, was the slim possibility I might have gotten pregnant. Because then the guards would have killed me and the baby. Or it would be my baby drowned in some filthy latrine.

All night every night I had to run back and forth to the latrine. On the way back from one trip I stopped and leaned against a wall. Every night I prayed "Please, Lord, we're all just pushing time here. Our lives have shrunk down to me, me, me and one more crumb of bread. Have one of these monsters shoot me in the back, I beg you."

The next day on my way back from the latrine I had to lean against the same wall. I was holding my stomach and crying because it was so sore from the disease. An older man came walking by, a new prisoner. He stopped and stared at me. I felt ashamed to be making such a spectacle but I couldn't stop crying.

He took his cap off and said, "My God, what can become of a human being! I knew your father, Benzion. I know what kind of home you come from. You had everything. Now you have to stand in this place like this. Wait here."

He went away and came back with a whole apple. He gave it to me and said, "Your father was a great man." Then he went away and I never saw him again.

The apple stabilized my system a little and that night I started thinking about my dad.

He was a little guy who started out with one horse cart and made a name for himself. He used his money to help people, especially the poor. He always brought strangers home and fed them and he supported a synagogue and several rabbis and scholars. When he walked to the synagogue to pray he ignored the Polish children and adults who threw rocks at him. He himself was so tolerant he let me have a little Christmas tree in the house because it gave joy to the maid.

I remembered the day he sat me down in my bedroom for a big lecture on the Maccabi sports club across the street from our house. I had just turned fifteen and he told me to never ever go near it. Apparently bad girls went there to flirt with boys. I had no idea what he was talking about. A ten-year-old today knows more about sex than I did when I got married.

This lecture just made me curious. I walked over to the club the next week and an older boy came up and started talking to me. Ten seconds later I felt a hand on my shoulder, my little daddy with his goatee. With his other hand he slapped me. I was astonished at this because he had never hit me before. In the camp that night I finally realized that he was just trying to protect me from the world.

The day the war started he came into my room for one last lecture. He squeezed my hands and said,

"Remember how I lived my life, Rose. Remember how important good deeds were to me." Good deeds was his whole philosophy of life. He used the Hebrew word: mitzvah. Then he left forever. He kissed my mother and went out the door into death.

I would not be here today if I didn't meet the man who brought me the apple and the memories of my father. Physically I was still weak but somehow those memories got me back on my feet again emotionally. I remembered how when my father sang and prayed at home I used to sing and pray with him. And those memories made me ashamed that I had prayed for the guards to shoot me.

Now when Pavlovska sneered at me I didn't care. And towards the end she was sneering all the time. In this last factory my forearms and face turned black from the metal powder that ground into our skin on the assembly line. My ribs stuck out and my hair was a clump. But my heart knew where it came from.

William's father Michael (Max) Schiff before
the war

William's mother Bertha and his sister Dorothy outside the family's barber-beauty shop

William's father Michael in front of the shop with his
employees and youngest son Bronek, left

Bronek, Dorothy, and William Schiff (left to right) in
Krakow, late teens

William's aunt Tonia Felczer did not survive. Here she wears a Star of David in the Krakow ghetto.

PROTOKOLL

aufgenommen am _7/8._ 1940.

In der Kanzlei der jüdischen Gemeinde in Krakau erscheinen: _Felczer Toni..._
Kraków

derzeit wohnhaft in Krakau _Josefa 12_ und die Zeugen:

a) _Berg Selati_ von Beruf _Buchhalt..._

wohnhaft in Krakau _Benedykta 11_ ausgewiesen durch _Ausweis_
Nr. J. ... Kraków Nr. 5699
ausgest 6 August 1940 and

b) _Felczer Zofia_ von Beruf _Kötschenauer..._

wohnhaft in Krakau _Josefa 18_ ausgewiesen durch _P. Ausweis_
Nr 49/F 1940 ausg. durch Magistr...
Kraków am 6/8 1940

Die Zeugen erklären folgendes: _Felczer Tonia_ geboren am _12/XI 1910_

in _Kraków_ Stand _Verheiratet_

Beruf _Hauswirtin_ aus _Kraków_

derzeit wohnhaft in Krakau _Josefa 12_

zuständig nach _____ ist uns persönlich bekannt.

Wir Bestätigen die Personengleichheit obiger Person mit untenstehendem Lichtbilde.

Obiges erklären wir, zwecks Erteilung eines Personalausweises von seiten der Jüdischen Gemeinde in Krakau in Angelegenheit der Umsiedlung des (der) Genannten von Krakau nach_____

Die Richtig... ...h bestätigen wir durch unsere eigenhändigen Unterschriften:

Schwarzer
Als Zeuge

Felczer Zofia
Als Zeuge

Felczer Tonia
Antragsteller

Everyone imprisoned in the Krakow ghetto had an official registration record. This is Tonia Felczer's, dated July 8, 1940.

William and Rosalie Schiff reunited in Krakow shortly
after the war with two relatives

The Schiffs with their son Michael in downtown Linz, Austria, 1948, shortly before leaving the Displaced Persons camp for the United States

William, Rosalie, and Michael Schiff on the deck of the USN *General LeRoy Eltinge*, somewhere off the coast of the United States in 1949

The Schiffs at the entrance to the Jewish quarter in Kazimierz in 1983. Left to right: daughter Rachel, grandchildren Jennifer and Michael, William, son Michael

In front of Rosalie's childhood family apartment/house in Krakow, 2002. Left to right: grandson Michael, William, granddaughter Jennifer

Auschwitz-Birkenau, 2002. Left to right: grandson Michael,
William, granddaughter Jennifer

Family trip to Poland, at the crematorium at Auschwitz. Left to right: son Michael, daughter Rachel, William, grandson Michael, granddaughter Jennifer, Rosalie, close family friends David Taub (also a survivor) and David's wife, JoAnn

Wedding of youngest granddaughter, 2005. Left to right: grandson Michael, son Bob, granddaughters Rebecca and Jennifer, Rosalie, daughter Rachel, William

Rosalie and William at the wedding of their youngest
granddaughter, 2005

chapter seven

Three days in the grave

The locomotive engineer who pulled his train off the camp spur at Auschwitz onto the main line three hours ago had a much simpler life before the Reich took the railroads over and painted swastikas on everything that rolled. The German train system had been the pride of Europe, 33,000 miles of beautiful tracks and 700,000 people with sane, productive jobs.

Twelve feet behind the engineer there's a loud rifle bang and a scream in the first open gondola car. He looks out at an overcast afternoon full of wicked gusty winds, neat farmhouses and snow-flocked trees. Twelve feet behind him another rifle goes bang and another wounded prisoner screams. He pulls back the throttle. Twenty kilometers an hour, twenty-one, twenty-two.

Crouching down in the rear corner of the first car, William watches a gut-shot prisoner squirm on the floor of the open wagon. The wounded man starts a fit of convulsions. A second bang punches a crude hole above his left eye and leaves him still. A third bang makes another standing prisoner jerk up like a marionette before he crumples in a heap. One hundred and four prisoners climbed into the gondola car three hours ago. At least twenty are dead, skulls spilling. Six SS sentries are shooting down into the car from their perches, one on each corner, two in the middle.

William knows the key to survival is avoiding eye contact. The prisoner who just fell like a puppet made a big mistake when he turned around to look up at the cruelest rifleman, the one in the left rear corner of the car who has killed half the dead men. To get out of this maniac's sight William slinks down low, takes a deep breath and crawls across the floor of the car directly toward the shooter. He wedges himself into the corner right under the muzzle of the gun and sits with his head slumped between his knees. Pulling a dark blanket over his head and shoulders he does his best to stay small and still.

> *This was the most frightening physical ordeal I went through during the war. The American army had just killed a quarter of a million German soldiers in the Ardennes and the Russians were chasing the Germans out of Poland. The SS men knew they had lost the war and we were fish in a barrel. This was their last chance to do what they loved best.*
>
> *You can't imagine the terror. Where do you hide from six rifles in such a small space? What good does hiding do when bullets go through one guy's neck into another guy's leg and then another guy's hand? People fall on top of you bleeding and shaking. This went on for three days. I couldn't see a thing with the blanket over my head so I felt like every bang was a bullet coming at me.*

The men in the thin pajamas are not just dying from bul-lets. Blankets give William a big advantage in the speeding open car.

> *During the evacuation from Auschwitz everybody pan-icked. This panic started two days earlier when we as-sembled for roll call and heard the Russian cannons in the distance. The Germans were trying to pretend that nothing was wrong but the boom-boom-boom kept get-ting louder and you could tell they were scared.*
>
> *Right after sunset that day the gangster came into the main room and made the big announcement. He said, "You have exactly one hour to put together what-ever you can carry for the journey. One hour starting now." We asked him where they were taking us. He said he had no idea.*
>
> *For sixty minutes everybody went crazy looking for food. It was twenty degrees outside and I was much more worried about the wind out of the north. So the first thing I grabbed were the three blankets that saved my life.*
>
> *One hundred and four people got into my gondola car; four got off at the next camp. I used a blanket to insulate my feet. The three other survivors got bad frost-bite. Their shoes froze to their feet. Two of them had to have amputations.*

As the camp dissolves, fires burn throughout the grounds. Administrators are burning files that document years of slaugh-ter. Prisoners scavenge while the wind wails and the Russian guns rumble. At midnight, January 18, 1945, the guards climb down from their watchtowers. Three and a half months after the mutineers blew up Crematorium 4, the Germans blast and topple the remaining chimneys. It is time for the Death Head soldiers to run.

Most of the 58,000 prisoners will be force-marched west until exposure and a bullet end their treks. William is one of the very few taken out on trains. Those left behind curse what initially appears to be the good luck of the men who end up in the rolling shooting galleries.

> *I just hid in the corner with my head down under the blankets. By the end of the first night maybe forty people were dead. Those bodies got tossed out into the snow during a stop. We started again and there was more shooting and screaming. Those bodies got dumped at a second stop. By nightfall on the second day the car was half empty.*
>
> *We never got food or water and everybody was crazy with thirst, shivering from the wind. At one point I heard somebody singing in German. The sound came from the direction of the locomotive and whoever it was sounded drunk.*
>
> *What kind of a person could sing at a time like this?*

At one point the train veers close to the town of Czestochowa. If it were not deadly for William to stand up and peer east, he could admire distinctive limestone mountain ridges on the eastern horizon. For two minutes he is only seventeen miles from the HASAG plant where Rosalie is making tank shells.

The engine pulls slowly west. The train has to stop from time to time when Allied planes are dropping bombs in its vicinity. On the morning of the third day the engineer sounds the long blast on his whistle. The train slows and stops and the sentry standing over the car littered with his victims hits William in the head with his gun barrel. "*Schnell, Judensau!* Move it, Jew-pig!"

This emergency dumping ground for evacuees is Gross Rosen, a vast stone quarry camp opened in 1940. Hitler and architect Albert Speer think the blue-gray granite from this region gives their monuments a timeless look. When Heinrich Himmler saw plans for hundreds of monuments the SS went into the rock business. The company Himmler put together, German Earth and Stone Works, needed slaves to work the granite veins. Forty thousand prisoners will die in the Gross Rosen quarry complex. Now the German retreat has crowded almost 100,000 prisoners into the camp. William is struck by the confusion.

> *We were being mixed together with new prisoners from all over Europe and everything was upside down. Everybody was speaking different languages and the Germans weren't even bothering to work us. In the morning we stood around for four hours. After an hour break we'd stand around another four hours before we went back to our bunks for the night.*
>
> *With all this time on my hands I tried to figure out a way to escape. At Auschwitz escape had been impossible, but at Gross Rosen, unlike Plaszow, I wouldn't be putting anybody else's life on the line.*
>
> *I noticed a small opening at the bottom of an*

*electric fence. Usually the Germans fixed things like
that right away but this time nobody bothered. Maybe
they thought that anybody skinny enough to squeeze
wouldn't have enough energy to try.*

He picks a cloudy night. When the camp is asleep he
ducks out the barrack door and pretends to head for the latrine. There are no dog teams or foot patrol. He takes a deep
breath, sprints twenty yards to the fence and flops down flat
on his belly. Rolling onto his back, he pokes his head out and
squeezes through the loose mesh, careful not to touch any
deadly humming wires.

One prisoner described the thick woods around Gross-
Rosen as a comforting bandage around an aching wound.
William finds the dense trees hard to run through in the
dark. His legs are pencil-thin and his clog shoes keep coming
off. He runs until burning lungs make him stop, then rests
until he can run again. He has no idea where he is going.
Emerging from the forest onto a country road, he traces it for
three or four hours until he hears voices and dives behind a
giant sycamore.

*I never saw these two farmers because I wanted to make
sure they didn't see me. Birds were starting to sing so
I could tell the sun was going to come up pretty soon.
These guys walked right past me without stopping. They
were Germans and I overheard a little bit of their conversation.*

*When they moved on it got lighter and I could see
a few farmhouses on either side of the road. Back in the
camp people warned me that escape was foolish because*

this was German territory. I thought surely not every German is a murderer. I knew the language pretty well by then and hoped that would count for something.

A truck went by with soldiers in the back and I was feeling real exposed in my striped pajamas. So I picked a nice-looking farm cottage. It had yellow stucco walls and a little wrought-iron fence in front. I opened the gate, walked up onto the porch, and let myself in.

A man and his wife were sitting at a table eating breakfast and listening to the radio. It's funny how the human mind works. Even in this situation I couldn't help noticing the radio. It was a neat modern design and I had never seen anything like it in the repair shop back in Krakow.

The couple were probably in their forties. The woman was a heavyset blond in a robe and her eyes got huge when she saw me. Like I was a ghost. Her husband was short with dark hair, dressed for farm work. He said, "You're a Jewish prisoner and you've escaped from the camp, haven't you?" Just like that, calm as could be. He asked me how I escaped and I told him. He said, "You ran all the way from the camp? You must really be exhausted!"

And he asked me to sit down at the table. His wife looked at him like he was crazy. He made her give me tea, a big bowl of lamb stew, and real bread that tasted like cake.

I told them my story the best I could without saying anything negative about Germans or Germany. That required a lot of tact. But I also told them truthfully how much I had always admired German culture and

*all the contributions Germany had made to the world.
I explained how I had defended their country in argu-
ments with my own father. I said every other diplomatic
thing I could think of.*

*When I was done eating the farmer promised me
he'd get me a change of clothes and figure out what else
he could do to help me. He said, "You look tired. Go lie
down and get some sleep."*

*His wife put an extra blanket on the bed for me in
a side room. I can't describe how it felt to lie down in
that bed. This was February 1945, five years and five
months since Poland was invaded. Suddenly I'm back
in a normal house that smells like apples and pears. I
tried to forget that when I was eating my second bowl
of stew I noticed one of those hero portraits of Hitler
on the wall over the radio. I knew that wasn't a good
sign.*

Thanks to the affordable People's Receiver radio, the
farmer has been long exposed to Hitler's views that Jews are
all perpetual plotters who promote ideas like brotherhood
and equality in order to trick simple honest people. So the
farmer doesn't think twice when a skinny Jewish prisoner
shows up at his door claiming to be a victim of history. With
the Russian army threatening to overrun his fields, the last
thing he intends to do is hide a smooth-talking terrorist who
just escaped from the local military base.

*When I woke up I heard them talking to soldiers on the
other side of the door. Three husky SS boys came charging in and pulled me out of bed. They threw me on the*

floor and stomped on me for a while. Then they tied my hands and threw me in the backseat of a car. We were back in the camp in ten minutes. I had a pistol barrel stuck in my ear the whole time.

The next morning the guards assembled the prisoners. They took off my pajama top and whipped me so bad I couldn't stand up for two days. The next day at roll call they made me stand in front of everybody with the same officer and a guard on either side of me.

The officer said, "This man tried to escape so today he digs his grave." Everybody watched me while I dug. We had all seen people dig their own graves before but it's a lot different when you're the one digging. I was weak so it took forever.

When the hole is about four feet deep, William's thin strips of back and bicep muscle can no longer lift the shovel blade over the edge.

They tied my hands and feet and laid me in the hole face up. I was sure they were going to shoot me in the face but instead they covered the hole with long planks. The earth was not cold but right away insects started crawling on my face and biting my neck and ears. It was completely dark until my eyes adjusted. A tiny crack of light between the boards helped me keep track of time.

I spent three days in the hole. I'd wake up with the bugs biting me and roll back and forth to shake them off and crush the ones under my clothes. I also rubbed my face in the dirt to scrape them off. I could have reached up and touched the boards, but I was afraid

*the guards would shoot me if they saw one move. It was
the usual situation—whatever you did was wrong. After
the second day I thought they were just going to leave
me there.*

Two hundred miles away Heinrich Himmler lies in bed
wondering what to do with countless numbers of buried Jews.
In February 1945 mass graves are one of his biggest problems.
The Allies are about to reclaim a lot of acreage where his
Death Head troops filled many giant holes with people. So far
he has done a fair job of concealing the evidence. Two million
bodies have been dug up in the last two years and burned by
special slave squads who carefully blend the ashes back into
the soil.

Himmler is proud of the way the Belzec death camp was
dismantled and plowed under. Wheat is growing on the site
and a passerby would never guess the Krakow Jews and more
than half a million other people died there. The last progress
report from Plaszow was positive, too. Eleven mass graves at
Goeth's camp gave up 9,000 putrefied bodies.

But with the Russians and Americans gaining ground so
fast Himmler knows he can't hide every corpse in Europe.
Not when a single camp like Treblinka killed almost 900,000.
Not when the total number of Jews is 6,000,000.

chapter eight

One hundred miles of rapists

The Jasna Gora monastery is not far from the HASAG plant where Rosalie now spits up blood every day. She and Mania chew their bread crusts close to the shrine of the Black Madonna in the monastery chapel. Art experts say the icon of the Virgin is the handiwork of a Byzantine master. Many Polish Catholics believe that Saint Luke painted the portrait of Mary while she was alive.

By Christmas 1944, the Nazis have murdered six Polish bishops and two thousand priests. Hundreds of plundered churches have been locked and seminarians must study in secret. Half a century later, one of these seminarians will ask the Jewish people to forgive Catholics for failing to help them during the Holocaust. Apologizing for wrongs the Church inflicted on Jews throughout the ages, Pope John Paul II describes the Holocaust as an indelible stain on the twentieth century and admits that centuries of Christian antisemitism may have facilitated the genocide.

Rosalie and Mania are too crushed by cruelty and cold to debate the history of hate. Frozen birds are dropping out of ancient oaks all across southern Poland and a typhoid epi-

demic is lending the Death Head soldiers a hand at the Czestochowa camp. More prisoners are dying in their sleep than
ever and the killers eliminate many more weaklings during
the morning cull. A new female officer prowls the barracks,
barging in unannounced to make the women jump.

"Who is sick here today?" she always yells. "Who has typhoid? Tell me!"

Nobody will give up names, so every morning she removes
at least one prisoner at random. This worries Rosalie because
Mania has been vomiting and having dizzy spells.

*One morning before roll call there was a surprise selec-
tion and the SS men were going through the barracks
systematically. We had never seen so many people involved at one time. I told Mania to get up, but she
couldn't do it. So I pushed her way back against the
wall in the shadows and covered her with a blanket.*

*When the guards came they dragged three or four
girls outside right away and started tearing all the blankets off the bunks. A young guard was approaching our
bunk and the only thing I could think to do was give
him a dirty look. I thought it might throw him off a
little because I was always very obedient. If I was too
offensive he'd shoot me, so I tried to make it more like
a quick disapproving glance. The guard called me a
whore and slapped me on the side of the head so hard I
saw stars. But he kept going, thank God.*

*We were all wasted down to nothing. On top of
all the blood I was spitting up I picked up another
case of dysentery, the kind where you lose blood in the
latrine. So in spite of my improved attitude it seemed*

like my hunch about not getting out of this camp was
coming true.

Pavlovska's personality changes as Christmas comes and
goes. For three days in a row the tall woman passes Rosalie's
workstation without mocking her or hitting her. Pavlovska's
husband has also lost his swagger. One afternoon he visits the
plant and pulls his wife out of earshot. She seems extremely
troubled as she absorbs his communication and Rosalie can
detect a new emotion on the ill-featured face.

"Fear. The bullies were traumatized because they knew the
Russians were coming. The next day I thought I heard thunder far away. Thunder in winter seemed strange. Then somebody said it was artillery. It kept getting closer and louder and
it gave Mrs. Pavlovska quite an anxiety attack. The last time
I saw her she was running somewhere and moving pretty fast
for such a big girl."

On January 15, 1945, the Germans force every slave who
can walk into boxcars. Rosalie can't find Mania and lacks the
strength to search. Losing so much blood has made her ane-
mic. "Towards the end I started to faint a lot. I would just pass
out and fall down and wake up on the floor with a bump on
my head."

She is on the floor of an empty barrack when a very young
regular army soldier shakes her shoulder. He is rounding up
the sick and Rosalie staggers with him from barrack to barrack as he collects the last girls in the camp. The soldier slowly
marches twelve weaklings into a big windowless warehouse
where a deep hole has been dug in the dirt floor. Shifting the
small machine gun slung across his shoulder, he tells them to
get down in the hole.

"We froze and held onto each other at the edge. I had been praying hard for the end but this wasn't what I wanted."

As the girls cower, the loudest artillery explosions yet shake the walls of the barn. The young soldier points to the hole and says, "You'll all be safer down there." They slide in and lie down on the dirt slopes. At sunset the Russian guns stop. At dawn the skylights in the roof turn white. Looking up, Rosalie sees the soldier leave. When he comes back half an hour later his helmet is off. He says, "We are lost, but for you comes a new life." Then he walks out, leaving the big door open.

I screamed to the girls behind me, "Did you hear what he said? What did he mean? What is happening?" One girl said, "It means we are going to be liberated." I pondered the word very carefully and thought the idea was impossible. I had seen lots of Jews go down into German holes before. I had put a lot of Jews in German holes myself. Nobody ever came back out.

I was absolutely expecting Pavlovska to run through the door laughing and pitch a few grenades in on top of us. That would not be out of character for the SS or for her. First, let's make the Jews think they're free, then we'll kill them.

We waited in the hole for an hour. The bravest girl finally crawled up and went over to peek out the door. She said, "I don't see anybody." The rest of us climbed to the top but we were still afraid a soldier would walk in and shoot us if we got out. That's how conditioned our minds were. We didn't have permission, you see. For five years we had needed permission to do the least little thing. To go to the bathroom, to stand up, to sit down.

After a while the brave girl went outside and we could hear her yelling her head off like a crazy person. "They're all gone! It's safe to come out! Come out! We're free!"

We went outside and when we saw the camp was empty we screamed and cried and hugged each other. Then we went to the main gate. This was also left open. We stood around for another hour. Who would give us permission to walk through this gate? Finally someone said, "They're not coming back. Let's go into town."

I was so weak I had to sit down in the dirt. That's when I saw the Russian soldiers. There was a long line of them walking up the road. When they saw us they started laughing and making what sounded like lewd jokes. I thought to myself, "Well, for an hour we were free."

None of these men seemed to speak Polish, but their officer kept them under control and tried to reassure us with gestures. They took over the camp hospital to treat their own wounded and carried me to a bed with other girls who could not walk. For the first few weeks they fed us and were very kind.

The Russian doctors gave us medicine and my stomach cramps and diarrhea subsided. I got to take a hot bath with soap and used up the whole bar. When I got out of the tub the water was black. The Russians burned my green skirt and William's jacket outside the infirmary window. When a little of the smoke blew inside it smelled like the body pit on the hill back at

Plaszow. And like boxcars. I will never forget the smell
of that burning skirt.

After two weeks we were nice and clean and had
fresh clothes. We smelled good and we looked better because we were eating and putting on a little weight.
This is when our troubles began.

The Germans had tortured us in every conceivable
way but we were usually safe from their lusts. Most of
them thought that sleeping with a Jewish woman would
be like sleeping with a dog. The Russian soldiers had no
such qualms. They had been away from their wives and
girlfriends for years. And they drank like fish.

So they started trying to trade us food for sex. Some
girls had more hunger than pride; the rest of us slept
four to a bed. This was good for safety, bad for sleeping,
and sleep was what I needed. The Russian doctor told
me the more sleep I got the quicker I would stop spitting
blood. I was worried about this because I kept fainting
all the time.

A Russian girl who had been a prisoner took pity
on me. She said, "My countrymen gave me my own
room. You can spend the night there tonight if you
want. You'll be safe, I promise." It sounded great so I
went to sleep in this room.

Sometime after midnight two Russian soldiers
kicked the door open. One jumped on top of me and I
got out of bed sideways like lightning. Then they tried to
trap me in a corner. Thank God the room was dark and
they were both extremely drunk. The one who jumped
on me fell over backwards when he climbed off the bed.
When he got back up he started singing:

It's a dark night
And we are here
And the war is over....

Then he said in pretty good Polish, "Come on, girl!
We gave you your freedom, now you need to give us
something." When they rushed around the bed to grab
me I jumped over it and ran out the door. There were
no guards up in watchtowers to shoot me this time so
I screamed my head off and woke up everybody in the
building.

The officer showed up and he had obviously just
jumped out of bed himself. The soldiers told him I lured
them into the room and offered them love for food. He
knew they were lying but he looked at me and shrugged
his shoulders. He said they were drunk and boys will be
boys.

The next day two other girls from Krakow and I
decided to leave before our luck ran out. Our hometown
was a hundred miles away but we felt our chances as
moving targets were better than the sitting duck situation in the hospital. Before we left I found a pair of
shoes in a closet. They were too small but they laced up
over the ankle. At least maybe I wouldn't get pneumo-
nia in the snow.

We walked out the main gate, afraid of our own
shadows. Every time we saw a horse wagon we hid in
the trees. Pretty soon we got to the main square of Czestochowa, a nice place with bakeries and candy shops
and other things we had forgotten. We tried our hands
at begging and found precious little charity. We dug
through garbage for scraps and started on our way.

It felt so strange to be walking down an open road without armed guards. If you wanted to stop and rest you could stop and rest. If you wanted to go right or left you were free to do so. This freedom didn't cheer me up much. Most of the members of my family were probably dead. The thought that William was dead, too—I just couldn't think that thought.

We picked our way through one town after another, very, very carefully. If we found a farm that seemed abandoned we'd dig for old potatoes and wipe the dirt off in the snow or eat them covered with dirt. You'd be surprised what you can eat when it's a matter of life and death. You would be appalled.

We started running into survivors who had been raped. There were new groups of soldiers in the area, even worse than the ones we left behind. They were hunting in packs for any woman they could find. We hid in fields and behind houses and barns. It was very hard to find any place to steal half an hour of sleep. How could we sleep after the stories the victims told? One eye was always open, all the way home.

The third or fourth night on the road we were inside a little barn when we heard soldiers outside, drunk and singing the same song:

> *It's a dark night*
> *And we are here*
> *And the war is over....*

We held our breath and hid between a cow and a horse. They kept us safe from the real animals.

chapter nine

A human being

Semi-comatose in the hole William hears a German voice:

"Now I'm going to show you what happens when you try to escape."

Fiery noon sunshine shocks his retinas as the guards toss the boards aside. The blinding flash of sky is interrupted by dark figures in helmets who reach down, grab him and jerk him back up into the world. Blinking, raw from bug bites, and covered with soil, he is too weak to stand. The soldiers hold him up for display in front of thousands of prisoners. When the officer tires of mocking him he is thrown on a bunk to die. A French Jew saves his life.

"He brought me soup for a few days until I got my strength back. I think he saw my escape as an act of resistance and assumed I was some sort of brave macho guy. He invited me to come to France after the war to start a new life. He said he would help me find a girl. I was touched because the French prisoners tended to stick to themselves."

Four days after William is unearthed the camp commandant announces that Gross Rosen will be evacuated. The Russian winter offensive refuses to slow down. With rockets and shells and wave after wave of punishment troops, the Soviet armies shatter anything that gets in their way. The SS keeps retreating and shipping prisoners west.

The news catches William off-guard. He knows he should start to hustle up food. Years in the camps have taught him that nimble anticipation is a big part of staying alive. As Gross Rosen evacuates he can't even walk without leaning on his new friend.

Forty thousand men march out of the granite quarry in early February. Most will trudge through the snow until they stumble and get shot. William's luck holds as once again he is among the few who get to ride a train. His French buddy boosts him up into another open gondola car.

William has a piece of bread for the journey, a chunk as big as his palm. This last-minute windfall comes from a prisoner he helped with food months earlier at Auschwitz. William remembers that when the man pulled the bread out of his waistband and pressed it into William's palm, he warned him to watch out for the Hungarians.

I don't want to say anything bad about the Hungarians. They suffered as much as the rest of us. But at this point prisoners were preying on each other. The strong stole from the weak. The Hungarians were the last Jews to be rounded up and they were healthier than people who went into the camps early. Some of them took advantage of this.

I was sitting on the floor of the train car holding onto my piece of bread. When I wasn't paying attention a little Hungarian boy jumped out of a corner and snatched it. A wild-looking kid with a dirty face, maybe

*ten years old. He stuffed the whole thing in his mouth
and jumped back into his daddy's arms. His dad was
a great big guy. He didn't say a word but he gave me a
look that said, sorry, that's life.*

Disinclined to retaliate and too weak to even stand up,
William packs five years of outrage and frustration into ten
minutes of shrieking, sobbing, and cursing.

"The French guy who thought I was such a hero could not
believe the tantrum I threw. At one point I was just yelling
Rose's name over and over. He seemed ashamed to sit next to
me on a train where other people were eating the dead."

As the locomotive moves further into Germany, three
Hungarians at the other end of the wagon start to butcher a
Greek. The man they hunker over was dead fifteen minutes
before they rolled him on his belly. They pull down his pajama bottoms and gouge into a gluteus muscle with a dull knife.
From William's vantage point a lot of sawing and yanking
seems to be required to get the stringy strips off the bone.

The wind has turned every face purple. Under a peak sun
the eaters' teeth and lips and fingers turn shiny red. Without blankets or bread William shivers violently in the open
wagon. The locomotive engineer sounds a long blast on the
whistle and the train slows and stops. William gets a gun barrel jab in the ribs from an SS man. Knowing what will happen
if he doesn't move, he pulls himself up and takes a look at
central east Germany.

On the nearby Ettersberg mountain the poet Goethe
once performed clever pantomimes to amuse a duchess in her
palace. One hundred and fifty years later the SS stage their
own productions in the mountain's shadow. At Buchenwald,

another camp designed to produce materials for Heinrich Himmler's German Earth and Stone Works, they harness prisoners to carts full of rocks and whip these "singing horses" down a road called Blood Street. Another diversion: tossing one Jew a day into a cage with a bear and an eagle. The bear dismembers the man, the eagle picks his bones. Sixty-five thousand inmates die here.

A guard warns the new prisoners that special machine guns in the watchtowers are rigged to fire automatically at any man who comes near the electric fence. The threat of robot weapons doesn't matter to William. The first week of rations will improve his health but his running days are over. In this place everyone's days look numbered. Skeletons hobble around and blink and wait to die.

> When jobs were assigned I got soup detail, which was like winning the lottery. When the guard called my name I cried for joy. Every day another prisoner and I got to carry the big pot of soup from the main kitchen to different barracks for distribution. We didn't have to stand in line and fight for food and I was getting my strength back.
>
> One afternoon we brought the empty soup pot into the kitchen and set it over in the dishwashing area. Out of the corner of my eye I saw a potato on the floor underneath a stove. More good luck, I thought. I grabbed it and hid it in my pants and when I was alone I ate the whole thing. There had been some dark mold or something on the skin that I tried to scrape off with a fingernail. This gave me some kind terrible food poisoning or dysentery.

A week of diarrhea and intestinal cramps strips away his last defenses. He is in such pain one morning he cannot lift the soup caldron and a guard pushes him away. He staggers back to his barrack and collapses on a bunk.

Heinrich Himmler has also collapsed on a bed at his head-quarters. The SS National Leader has been busily trading Jews for a chance to save himself. More than half a year earlier his secret agents offered to free a number of Jewish prisoners for Allied trucks and other supplies the German army needed desperately to stop the Russian offensive. That deal fell through, but now Himmler has gone behind Hitler's back again, releasing convoys of prisoners to the International Red Cross.

He thinks he has a chance to negotiate a peace with the western leaders. He knows the Americans don't want Stalin to end up with most of Europe. And he assumes they will need a hand controlling the German people after the war. To convince them he can help, he must first shed his reputation as the greatest mass murderer in history. If setting a few Jews free is what it takes, he is willing to ignore Hitler's recent order to kill every prisoner and slave in the camp system. He has instructed his agents to fatten more Jews with decent food in case they are needed as poker chips.

The last few months have been hard on Himmler. When Hitler sent him into Poland to stop the Russians, he badly bungled his attack against Russian field marshal Georgy Zhukov, perhaps the greatest tank commander in history. Soldiers whom Himmler swore would fight like lions fled pell-mell from the counter-attack. In the Chancellery building back in Berlin, Hitler screamed at Himmler in wild fury, blaming the SS National Leader for ruining a war that started out so well the day the first Special Forces rolled into Poland.

In addition to his usual headaches and stomach problems, Himmler now has heart pains. These secret negotiations with the enemies of the Reich are the trickiest business he has ever attempted. If the Fuhrer finds out he will be shot for treason. It is traumatic for the SS National Leader to turn on his messiah. Having broken his sacred oath of loyalty he lies in bed wincing from angina.

At Buchenwald William aches in his bunk. The boards are hard on his meatless shoulder blades and tailbone and spine. He cannot sleep on his side because the boards hurt his knobby shoulder joint and the exposed ridge of his pelvis. Buchenwald is a dying camp and that's what the bicycle repairman is doing. Why he is dying he will never understand. Every day since the war began he has tried to unravel the absurdity of the matter. No glimmer of sense emerges.

Is he really going to die because he happened to be born a Jew in a wild jungle called Poland? Is that why his bride is missing in action and everybody else went into the fire? Simply for belonging to the same religion? This is why the Germans killed his father? A man who believed in nothing?

The mother he loved more than anything in the world was a believer. She had a rabbi bless him the day he was born and she sent her son to Torah school. The rituals never meant much to him. He was a modern boy at heart through and through. Bicycles and radios and girls were more interesting than Hebrew. But to keep his mother happy he put on the prayer shawl and prayed.

Once the Nazis came, it was for his mother he stuck his neck out to make sure there was always a chicken in the house for Sabbath dinner. Human lives depended on all his smuggling runs, but for some reason the Sabbath birds seemed to have a value beyond their nutritional flesh and fat. He cannot forget the chicken that suffocated on the way back to the ghetto from the market shed, the only bird that ever smothered under his coat.

He laid the four-pound hen on the table in the shoebox ghetto apartment. Not fifteen minutes had passed since life left the body, but his mother's starving Orthodox friends turned up their noses. Under no circumstance would they feed their starving children such meat. Not when the Torah explicitly warns: "When one of the animals you could otherwise eat, dies of itself, anyone who touches its dead body shall be unclean..." The sense of his religion was not shining brightly for William that particular afternoon. When the Germans murdered his mother it seemed to have no validity at all.

Immobilized on his bunk, he remembers the day she solved a dilemma that soured his life unexpectedly at age seventeen. Sensing her son's anxiety, Bertha asked him what ate at his heart. Eight years before Buchenwald he told her his trouble.

His best friend at this time was from an Orthodox family, and the two young men rode bicycles together almost every day. This friend had a good-looking girlfriend, who had been raised an orphan. One fall morning all three took a bicycle trip in the countryside with a group of friends. William had a brand new bike that far outclassed the others and made a deep impression on his friend's girl. She asked endless questions about it and wanted to ride it and seemed to need a lot of help getting on and off. The next week his friend came to the bike shop with a request.

"William," he said, "will you do me a favor? My girlfriend doesn't like to be alone on Saturday but I have to be with my family. She was wondering if you could keep her company so she doesn't get lonely."

The next weekend William and the girl rode into the country alone. She brought blankets in case the two might need to rest and taught him how to kiss on those blankets. The girl started coming to the bike shop every day. Word got around and his friend showed up at the shop. He said, "William, why are you doing this?"

"Because you asked me to," William said.

"You need to stop," his best friend insisted.

"I'm trying," he said, "but I don't think I can."

The friendship ruptured and the girl proved hard to hold onto. From time to time she disappeared for days and William grew suspicious. The thought of her kissing other boys made it impossible for him to eat or sleep. He tailed her through the streets of Krakow like a detective. In these same streets he often saw his friend. The burden of guilt and jealousy was crushing him until his mother illuminated the situation.

"You had a good friend," she said, "and now you have a girl who is everyone's friend and nobody's friend. It's hard to do the right thing, William, but that's what good men do."

Five years after she spoke those words, Heinrich Himmler's men put her in the fire because of her religion. If it made any sense he would cry. Immobilized on his bunk he doesn't have the energy. He passes out until someone calls his name.

> *I looked out of my bunk and saw a big tall bald guy filling up the whole door. He says, "William, is that you? Don't you remember me? I was in your barrack at Auschwitz and I worked in the lab with Dr. Meisel."*

This guy was a chemist who worked in the section that developed serums. He took one look at me and knew I didn't have long to live. He was about forty then and I was twenty-six and he rescued me like a big brother. First he spoonfed me water, then soup.

He told me, "Listen carefully and we'll both live through this war. We get so little bread each day we can't eat it all right away. We have to regulate our food intake to keep our energy levels stable. We'll each break our bread into three pieces. Then we'll both eat one piece for breakfast, one piece for lunch and one piece for dinner. Trust me, this will improve our chances."

The next morning he divided his bread into three pieces and did the same with mine. We put all six pieces of bread on the edge of my bunk. Then we started the experiment with the morning ration. He said, "Chew it slowly."

I ate the first piece nice and slow. It was raining hard that day and you could look out the door and see the camp ground turning into a giant mud puddle. He sat on the floor with his back against the bunk and talked a lot to help pass the time.

It did my spirit good to listen to all his plans for after the war. He was from Vienna and wanted to go home and become a professor. He wanted to have a family and publish papers and so on. He was an intellectual. An idealistic man, full of life.

I was so torn up with hunger I ate my second piece of bread before the first hour was up. He saw me reach out and grab it, but he didn't scold me because he didn't want to hurt my feelings. He didn't say anything an hour later when I ate my last piece. And he didn't say anything when I ate his second piece of bread. It was a terrible thing for me to do, but I couldn't stop myself. He saw me do it and he kept right on talking.

It rained all morning while he painted a bright picture of the future and kept encouraging me to be optimistic. At supper time, which was two o'clock in Europe, he reached for the last piece of bread. I had been craving this little crust for hours. It had taken all my self control to keep from grabbing it and shaming myself again.

He raised it to his lips and was just about to put it in his mouth. Then he stopped. I know my eyes must have been bugging out of my head staring at that piece of bread. He must have felt my eyes because he put the bread in my hand. Then he started talking again about how much he loved Vienna.

A lot of prisoners said they did heroic things in the camps. I have heard ridiculous tales of espionage and weapons smuggling. I never did anything heroic myself and the whole time I was in the system this man was the only hero I ever saw. The Germans spent years trying to reduce him to an animal, but he kept his heart clean to the very end, when other prisoners were strangling each others for crumbs and some people were abandoning members of their own family.

This man gave his whole life to me. To a virtual stranger. Like it was nothing. That is what it means to be a good person. That is what it means to be a human being. I was so touched I couldn't take it. I had to give it back.

At roll call the next day the camp administration announces another evacuation. All rations have been cancelled. There will be no more bread. The chemist tells William to wait in his bunk while he tries to scare up some food. Far away, the Russian guns start booming and Buchenwald devolves into chaos.

In his bunk William could not care less. He drifts in and out of consciousness and loses track of time. Guards shove able-bodied men out the door. Only the bed-bound are left behind. One guard gives William a funny look as he leaves.

"It seemed he was making a mental note to himself—*there's one we'll have to come back and take care of.*"

Half an hour later the sharp crack of pistols starts next door.

> *I heard a scream and I knew right away that the mop-up squad was liquidating people. Before I heard the scream it was an effort just to breathe. But when shooters are coming your way it's a tremendous motivator. I crawled out the door on my hands and knees.*
>
> *They were shooting in the barracks to my right and left. Either way you went you were dead. All the barracks were raised on blocks so I crawled straight underneath the building as far as I could and lay there hiding while the camp evacuated. The next day it was quiet. I would pass out for hours and wake up for just a few minutes.*
>
> *On the third day death was very close. I was paralyzed and felt completely hollow inside. Then I heard a strange language. I tried calling for help but could only make a moaning noise. Two American soldiers crawled under and pulled me out. They took me to the camp hospital and put me on a scale. I weighed sixty-nine pounds. When Hitler invaded Poland I weighed a hundred and eighty-five.*

chapter ten

Ghost town

Against a late afternoon sky full of dark snow clouds Rosalie spots the three towers of Wawel castle. She has hiked a hundred miles in shoes that keep her feet dry but make her toes bleed. Three miles outside the city, she and her companions stop to rest.

"We had to prepare ourselves for what wouldn't be there."

One thousand years earlier, a Jewish merchant from Spain walked into town past the same spot where the girls sit shivering. Krakow was unknown to history until he took up a pen to describe the place as a center of commerce. Poland converted to Christianity the very next year.

The girls get up and trudge towards Wawel Hill, where men have lived for at least 12,000 years. The first inhabitants left stone weapons behind; later encampments traded with Nero's empire. When the Vistulan tribe showed up, legends say their chief built his fort where the Renaissance castle stands today.

Krak was the name of this mythical king, the ruler plagued by Smoke, the child-eating dragon. In real life, the Germani tribe were the most dangerous predators in the Vistulan domain. Rather than marry one of these arrogant invader chieftains from the west, Krak's daughter Wanda supposedly drowned herself in the river.

After the age of legends Mongol invaders came from the east and razed Krakow. The citizens built another boomtown with mail coaches that ran all the way to Italy. In subsequent centuries a German tyrant tried to tear the walls down and failed. The Swedish army came and tore them down with ease. Napoleon grabbed the city for four years. A czar took it back.

Decade after decade, Russians, Prussians, Austrians, and fresh generations of Germans played kickball with Rosalie's hometown. Exhausted by occupiers, the citizens declared themselves an independent republic. Their reward was a century of fiercer occupations.

Throughout 12,000 ruthless years no invaders had been as inhuman as the Nazis. Fleeing the dragon castle where he supervised the murder of 70,000 Krakow Jews, Hans Frank said he was sorry he had no time to dynamite every shrine and synagogue.

Rosalie and her friends stand in the stone plaza of the Jewish Square. When they were children, vendors thronged this market singing out the virtues of their wares. Now, under a dark sky, three scrawny orphan girls cringe in the empty market against a wind full of stinging sleet.

I thought to myself, why did we ever come back here? The memories started to hound me right away. All the blood had been washed off the streets but in my mind I could still see it everywhere. There was a silence, a vacuum of humanity you could feel.

This was especially true in my old neighborhood
of Kazimierz. The buildings remained but the people
were gone. They had all been replaced by strangers. You
would look through the window where a friend once
lived and new people were sitting around your friend's
old dining room table. These newcomers were eating off
your friend's old china and relaxing on her sofa.

Seventy thousand people, all gone. To erase people,
to murder them, is wicked. To replace them, to casu-
ally transfer their homes and possessions to newcomers,
is a strange form of evil.

Up and down the streets of Kazimierz she searches for
anybody who might have news of William or her father. The
Orthodox peers of Benzion Baum, the men he used to pray
with and the Torah scholars he supported, have vanished. In
Cossack Square she knocks on the door of the private prayer
house built by her dad's best customer, the man who owned
the candy and shoe polish factories. Up and down Jozefa and
Grodska streets, up and down Meiselsa Street, she knocks on
many prayer house doors.

Nobody.

All the men in long black coats with white beards flowing
out from under black fur hats are gone. The bookstores run
by the Tafet and Sieden families, always crowded in the past,
are closed. So is the Jewish Theater. No boys and girls mingle
in the park outside the Maccabi sports center. The Jewish Stu-
dent Dormitory that held so many important art exhibitions
and the old folks home on Skawinska Street are both empty.

Rosalie and her friends are among the first of only 1,000
Jews who will return to Krakow. For lack of any place else

to go they gravitate to the "new" synagogue built in 1553. The Germans turned this place into a warehouse for body bags and the door is locked. But the wall protecting the sacred space behind the building has been torn down. The girls step over the rubble of the wall and enter the Old Cemetery.

Since the occupation began, the sloping yard has been used as a garbage dump and vandals have broken almost all the tombstones. Among the old gnarled trees only a dozen or so moss-covered markers still poke through the snow. At the foot of one tree the slab of the most famous rabbi in Poland stands intact, decorated with carvings of a thickly clustered grapevine under a crown that symbolizes wisdom. Rosalie's Hebrew is good enough for her to scan the epitaph of Moses Isserles:

> *A great scholar, the light of the West...*
> *...spreading knowledge among the people...*

On other stones there are symbols. A deer, a pitcher, a blessing hand, stylized blossoms, and the sea creatures called Leviathans. The medallion on Keila Ezriel's tombstone bears the zodiac image of Capricorn. A pair of scissors shows that Isaac Schneider was a tailor. There is Gershon Heller, the Talmud expert who called his autobiography *The Scroll of Hatred*. There is Michael Kalahora, whose father was burned at the stake for blasphemy against Christianity. Another worn inscription:

> *Our joy has turned into sorrow,*
> *the honor of Israel has been taken away,*
> *the crown has fallen from our head...*

Using the tombstones as windbreaks, the girls huddle together with their backs against the wall of the Remuh. All
around them, under the snow and garbage, lie smashed names
like Golde, Dobrosh, Drezel, and Malka, daughters buried
long before the Jews of Poland began to mix deliberately with
the local population.

In different ways, William and Rosalie's parents held onto
the old traditions. But they were also part of a new generation that took an active part in Polish society. During the
nineteenth century Krakow Jews emerged as patriots and city
leaders. In 1900, they were ten times more likely to be businessmen than the general population. By the early thirties
more than half the Jews in the city had left Kazimierz to move
into Christian neighborhoods. The new visibility and upward
mobility caused problems.

The year before Hitler invaded Poland, Krakow newspapers seemed more concerned with "the Jewish invasion" of
the local real estate market. It was considered a great indignity
that the old homes of local nobles were being bought by Jewish investors. The anger and envy is plain to see six years later
when the sun finally shines on the garbage-covered graves and
the broken daughter of the businessman Benzion Baum.

"I suppose the local people resented us for doing well," Rosalie says. "Mom and I certainly got a big surprise when we
asked one of Dad's employees to hide my little brother. My father fed this man's family for twenty years and we considered
him a loyal friend. He looked at Henry, a little child, and said,
'Why should I stick my neck out for this dirty Jew?' None of the
sixty men on Dad's payroll offered to help us in any way."

The girls don't dare risk a second night out in the open.
They take refuge in the Basilica of the Virgin Mary in Krakow's

central square. There they sleep on hard pews surrounded by the crypts of dead burghers.

"When I was a child our maid Maria would take me into the city to visit the dress shop my aunt owned. On the way back she would always duck into this church to pray. I never imagined that ten years later I would be sleeping on the same benches."

When the morning bells ring at St. Mary's, acolytes appear beneath the gothic altarpiece to make ready for mass. The survivors rub their eyes and prepare to hunt food.

We were street people. We waited outside shops and restaurants hoping to find something to eat in the garbage. For two or three weeks we scrounged and begged like this. One afternoon it was already getting dark around four o'clock and we could find nothing. I had been coughing and spitting up blood so bad I thought I must have tuberculosis.

The wind off the river was cutting through us and somehow we ended up on Dietlovska Street. All of a sudden I'm looking up at bright yellow lights in the windows of the home where I grew up. The emotion was overpowering. I said to myself, "That's my house. Why am I dying out here?"

I couldn't stand the cold or the loneliness or being sick any more. I started crying and I felt this impulse. I knew it would be the hardest thing I had ever done but I thought, "Please, God, for the last time, hear my prayer and help us."

The girls and I went creeping up the stairs. I knocked on the door and a Polish woman opened it.

Behind her I saw all my parents' furniture, every stick. The same big mirror on the wall. The same black and red carpet on the floor.

"I'm sorry to bother you," I said. "This used to be my family's home before the war. My friends and I have come a long journey on foot from a concentration camp. I don't want to reclaim anything but we're freezing and I'm sick. All we need is a place to rest until the storm is over."

She got a vicious look on her face and yelled, "Get out, dirty Jews!" Then she slammed the door. For me, you know, emotionally, this was the end of the road. The ghetto I survived. Amon Goeth, Pavlovska, many other things. Now the woman sleeping in my dead parents' bed tells me to go freeze to death in the street.

When my friends and I turned to go, there was a lady on the landing who overheard the conversation. She said a college professor lived upstairs with rooms he was trying to rent, a poor man but with a heart. We went upstairs and knocked on his door and told him our story.

He said, "Because you've been in a camp I want to give you a roof over your head. We aren't getting our salaries at the university so I can't help with food. I don't even have money for firewood. But at least you'll be out of the elements."

That night the girls and I slept on the floor in the kitchen of this kind man. He is dead now but if I could see him today I would kiss both his hands. Not all the Polish people were bad. It is very important to remember that fact.

There was only one sad note in the arrangement for me. This apartment was once the home of my father's friend and the home of my sister's best friend. That night we slept on the kitchen floor of Mania's apartment. I dreamed I saw her walking down a road all alone, barefoot in the snow.

As more survivors trickle back a registration office opens in the old Jewish Community Center. Rosalie checks every day for news. Scrutinizing the roster one afternoon, she is approached by a stranger recently arrived from Russia. He is ten years her senior, well-dressed, and looking for a room to rent. She recommends the professor and introduces the men.

A few Jews made a lot of money in Russia during the war. David was one of these black market wheeler-dealers. He took a room, paid the professor several months rent in advance and was very generous to me and the girls. He bought blankets and firewood and he shared food. We were beside ourselves with joy. We still slept in the kitchen, but now at least the kitchen was warm and there were regular meals.

David seemed to favor me and I was getting pressure from my friends to be nice to him. They didn't want to dig through any more garbage. It was at this time I remembered some advice my grandmother Sarah gave me when I was growing up. "Rosalie," she used to say, "never tell a man how much you eat. If you want an extra little meal now and then, that's your secret."

She told me this half a dozen times and always chuckled like it was some kind of divine mischief. When

*David hired me to do his shopping and cooking it popped
back in my head. Before I came home I made it a point
to eat some of the food I bought in the market. Later I
ate the regular meal with everyone else. Thanks to all
this secret snacking my health improved rapidly and so
did my figure.*

*My friends and I were going out one night with a
girl I met at the registration office. She was having a
little birthday party at her apartment, but David wanted to know when I was coming home and if other men
would be at the party. I told him those were questions
my husband could ask, nobody else.*

*From that night forward he became very possessive.
He sent my friends to do all the shopping so I could stay
home and concentrate on the more serious business of
cooking. This was so laughable. I couldn't cook to save
my life. When David confined me to the kitchen I just
chopped vegetables and pretended I knew what I was
doing until the girls got back to help.*

*On the anniversary of my mother's deportation I
cried all day. David held my hand and told me I needed
to forget about the past. He said the best way to do that
was to start thinking about the future. What he wanted me to do was to forget about William. David was
a smart guy but a conniver. He was not a good-looking
man to start with, but really it was this weasel quality
that made him so unattractive. Not that it made any
difference. I was waiting for William, period.*

William is on a train again, seated properly for a change
in a covered passenger coach. Beside him sits his good friend

and patron Dr. Meisel, the serum expert from Auschwitz. They are bound for Breslau, the first major station en route to Krakow.

> *In Buchenwald the GIs took me to the hospital and fed me intravenously for four days. This was more good luck. Almost half the prisoners died when the GIs gave them solid food. They gorged until their stomachs burst. It was such a sad thing for them to starve for years and then be killed by plenty.*
>
> *I woke up in the hospital one morning and there was Dr. Meisel sitting in a chair by my bed. He got to Buchenwald the hard way, walking in the snow, and he still wanted me for a son-in-law. I said we'd have to find out what happened to Rose before I could even think about it. After ten days of real food I could walk again. After seven more weeks I fleshed out and was ready to go.*
>
> *In the hospital the Red Cross gave all of us new clothes and I ended up with a crazy-looking Cossack outfit. Baggy pants, a white blouse with long puffy sleeves, a short heavy brown coat and funny little shoes. Dr. Meisel laughed hard when he saw me.*
>
> *When we got on the train to Breslau the Russians had painted over all the signs. Where it used to say, "No Dogs or Jews" now it said, "No Dogs or Germans." We thought this was great justice until two German ladies got on board. Dr. Meisel spoke Russian and heard two newly released Russian POWs. These guys were planning to toss the women over a bridge while the train was moving. They had been through hell in the camps, too, and they were out for revenge.*

Sure enough, when the train approached a bridge they started dragging the women toward the back of the car. This was a middle-aged female and her teen-aged daughter, both nicely dressed, minding their own business. The girl screamed because one guy was yanking her down the aisle by the hair. This made her mother doubly hysterical.

Dr. Meisel got up and asked the men to show some mercy. For a minute the mother was in the middle of a tug-of-war. The Russian was jerking on her left arm while Dr. Meisel held the right arm and I held him. It made quite a spectacle for the other passengers.

We stalled things until the train crossed the bridge. The second it pulled into the station the Russians threw all four of us off. One of them spit on me and called me a name. Dr. Meisel laughed and said, "He just called you a German-lover."

Ejected three miles outside Breslau, the men escort the assault victims up a road into town. They have scarcely taken leave of the German women when a Jewish girl greets them like family.

We were standing in the street and this pretty kid, maybe seventeen, came running up out of nowhere. She started hugging both of us and saying how good it was to see us after all these years. I could tell she was a survivor and thought she might be mentally ill.

Then I saw the big Russian soldier following after her. This guy was tall as a tree and also very young. He wasn't vicious but she told us he'd been courting her ag-

gressively for the past few days. When he walked up to us she said: "This is my brother and my uncle. They've come to take me back to our home in Krakow and we need a place to stay."

His duty was to keep order in the streets of Breslau and he could do whatever he wanted. After what the German soldiers did to Russian civilians none of these guys had any sympathy for the locals. He walked us straight up the nicest street in town, waved his hand at all the gorgeous houses and told the girl to take her pick.

She chose a three-story stone villa, like a mansion in a movie. The kid pounded on the door and told the Germans they had thirty minutes to get out. As they were leaving, the woman gave Dr. Meisel a dirty look.

"You should be ashamed of yourself," she said. "We have children."

He said, "Your kids are alive. This isn't even a whiff of what we went through."

This particular Russian soldier was a wonderful guy, very well mannered. He told me he desperately wanted to marry my sister and promised he would take good care of her. He told two different restaurant owners to feed us night and day, whatever we wanted to eat, and not expect to be paid. There was no grumbling. In the camps we obeyed the men with the rifles and so did the Germans in occupied Breslau.

One afternoon I met another girl I knew from before the war. She was leaving for Krakow. I asked her to see if Rose had made it back to Dietlovska Street. We stayed three weeks in Breslau while Dr. Meisel

*tried to find some people he knew. I started to feel a
lot better.*

*When Dr. Meisel was ready I told my make-believe
sister we had to leave. That night she knocked on the
door of my room. The villa had many rooms and it
seemed like every bedroom had a big canopy bed. She
said she needed to talk and told me she didn't really
have any family left in Krakow. Everybody was already
dead. She was afraid of the Russian boy and needed
someone she could trust to look after her. Then she
started crying.*

*There were so many people in Europe, millions of
them, trying to scratch some kind of life together out
of the dirt. I told this poor girl I had to find Rose. She
said Rose was probably already married to another man
and might even have a child by now. I said that was
something I needed to make sure of myself.*

*When she said Rose was probably dead I rejected
the idea. For two and a half years, ever since I got on
the train to Auschwitz, I had been thinking about Rose.
I thought about her every minute I wasn't thinking
about food or getting killed. She was just a kid when I
met her. She thought the stork brought babies and our
honeymoon night was very special. I had to find her
again. It was my duty.*

On their last night in Breslau the three survivors lie in different canopy beds pondering the future. Back on Dietlovska
Street, Rosalie still sleeps in a cramped kitchen where she can
no longer chop vegetables without interruptions.

David started making passes. Not ugly passes, really, just trying to kiss my hand all the time. I could tell we were going to have trouble because he trembled so much when he did this. He had lost a lot of family, too, so there's no telling what kind of psychological trauma he was dealing with. All of us had problems but his got out of control.

He cornered my girlfriends and told them they should talk sense to me and convince me to marry him. He said it was ridiculous that a girl from a family like mine should be married to a poor guy like William. David was a terrible snob and for this he lost all my sympathy. Then he tried to badmouth William to me directly. He said, "Why are you still waiting for that nobody?" I told him, "If it wasn't for that nobody you'd be kissing a dead girl's hand."

It blew up when the girls and I came home from a second little party. David and the professor were sitting at the dining table and both had obviously been drinking. David went into a rage and went into his bedroom and came out with a little suitcase full of gold and zloty notes and shook it out all over the floor in front of me. He said he was going to kill himself and ran into his room and slammed the door. We could hear him sobbing and we all felt bad for him.

The professor and my friends kept staring at the money. They had never seen so much cash before. All I saw was a rug that used to belong to Mania's family. The next day I told David it was okay if he wanted to leave. I told him he didn't have to keep feeding us. My girlfriends were listening in the

*kitchen, scared to death. He apologized and said
he'd behave himself.*

Every day Rosalie continues to check for news. One day a
walking skeleton enters the registration office. He had been at
Buchenwald, evacuated from the same barrack where William
was left behind. When he hears Rosalie mention William's
name he reluctantly tells her the SS liquidated every strag-
gler.

*I fainted on the floor and had to be carried back to the
apartment. Again, David did his best to comfort me
while trying to hide his joy. I didn't eat anything for a
week but one morning I told myself I had to come to
grips with reality and get on with my life. I got dressed
and went downstairs for some fresh air.*

*When I crossed the street a strange woman ran up
to me and asked me my name. When I told her she got
all excited and said, "I just came from Breslau! I saw
William there! He'll be home any day!" This time I
fainted in the middle of Dietlovska, right in between all
the horse wagons.*

*That night in the apartment we had a celebration
party and my friends made me drink some of the professor's whiskey, the first and last time I ever tasted such
horrible stuff. David couldn't hide his anger now but
it was my turn to make a scene so I threw the whiskey
bottle at him.*

*I went to the registration office and waited every
day. I had my own little table and chair in a corner.
Four or five days I waited. No William. Each night*

*I went home disappointed, praying nothing had hap-
pened to him on the way. The last night I walked home
past the park where the two Polish boys tried to trip me.
It seemed like another life entirely.*

*When I got back to the apartment building I was
walking up the staircase very slowly. David was sulk-
ing upstairs and I was in no hurry to deal with that.
I ran my hand along the banister. My dad used to get
mad because I loved to slide down it when I was young.
"Rose!" he'd shout down to me, "are you a boy or a
girl? Rose! Do you want to grow up to be a woman or a
man?"*

*I was thinking about the way my father's voice used
to echo in the stairwell when he shouted out my name
like that. And all of a sudden I heard another voice
shouting out my name. It was not the voice of a dead
man.*

"Poor David," William recalls. "The night I showed up
at Dietlovska Street dressed like a Cossack Rosalie fainted on
the stairs. David had to help me carry her up to the apartment
and he wasn't happy when she woke up and we started kissing."

chapter eleven

On the border

"It is not true that I or anyone else in Germany wanted war in 1939. It was desired and instigated solely by international finance conspirators of Jewish blood or working for Jewish interests."

In his suicide note Adolf Hitler tried to shift the blame for the six years of pain he forced on the world by invading Poland. The day before he dictated the note he learned that Heinrich Himmler had betrayed him. A radio brought the news down into the bunker. When Hitler heard that Himmler was trying to negotiate a separate peace he screamed until his face turned brownish purple. The thinker of the new Germany had finally been abandoned by his doer, the man who translated hate into bodies.

Himmler killed himself three weeks later. After the Allies spurned his absurd diplomatic overtures his last days were desperate. Of the 800,000 elite killers he commanded in his prime, only two nervous aides remained. Forced to drive his own bulletproof car, the SS National Leader promptly ran it into a ditch. He shaved his moustache, donned an eye patch, and disguised himself as a sergeant. When the British caught him and stripped him down to his underpants he sneered at the burly sergeant who ordered him into his jail cell.

It was the last order he ever obeyed. Once it became clear that he would face a judge he shook loose the capsule of cyanide hidden inside a molar. Fear of the noose made him bite through the glass. He had seen a lot of hangings. After his death a reporter asked his wife about the SS National Leader's reputation as evil incarnate. She shrugged her shoulders: "He was a cop. Nobody likes cops."

A few other diehards went down defiantly. Paul Budin knew that no Allied judge would accept his excuses for HASAG's murder of 60,000 work slaves. The war CEO and his socialite wife died when Budin blew up the company's main office in Leipzig. And Plaszow commandant Amon Goeth gave a stubborn Nazi salute when a Polish tribunal hanged him. During his trial he objected that Poles had no right to judge a German in the first place. When it came to specific charges he denied facts and blamed other soldiers.

In one of Goeth's last blood orgies at Plaszow he shot Jewish police chief Willek Chilowitz, William's old girlfriend Marysia, Mietek Finkelstein, and all the other top police captains. He showed the bodies on the dirty campground so prisoners could marvel at the flies in their mouths.

As the Reich crumbled, worker bees like Pavlovska tossed their swastikas and faded into the crowd. In later life she may have argued that she was a victim of dehumanization training and factory managers who gave her direct orders to grind the slaves. She may also have blamed Berlin and her fellow countrymen. After the Nazi takeover, almost everyone signed off on the program either by saluting or remaining silent. When the party said it was time for preemptive strikes against any new attack the Jews might be plotting, Pavlovska and millions of other citizens felt they had to believe this to be good Germans.

In summer 1945 William and Rosalie are on the road together, trying to hitch a ride out of Poland. William will not miss the storybook castle on Wawel Hill.

The first week I came back I went to my father's salon. When the Nazis made it illegal for Jews to own a business Dad made an arrangement with his most trusted employee. We legally transferred the business to this guy for a few bucks with the understanding that my family would get our shop back after the war.

When I walked in he was shaving a customer. He was friendly until I reminded him of the agreement. Then he got ugly and started shouting. "I paid for it! It's mine!" And he dared me to take him to court. The communists were in charge now so I knew better than to bother. Instead, I went to visit the wall-paneling factory that Rosalie's dad built. One of his original partners offered me a great job, but by this time Rose had had it. She said, "People around here aren't going to change any time soon. Take me someplace where I can live my life in peace."

And I'm glad she talked me into it because in August right after we left there was an anti-Jewish riot. Some malicious gossip started a rumor that Jews were kidnapping little Christian children and draining their blood to use in religious services. In the great new age of radio and airplanes ridiculous old superstitions like this were still getting people killed. Three hundred innocent Jews like us were murdered this way the first year after

*the war. We didn't leave Krakow because the winters
are hard. We ran away from hate.*

William's childhood friend Benny, another camp survivor, accompanies them on the road. His father had been a milk man who loved to let neighborhood kids ride on his wagon through the streets of Kazimierz. William can trust Benny with anything, but he remembers Rosalie's former suitor David as persistent to the end.

> *David moved out but he never really got the message.
> He'd hang around in the street pouting. The morning
> we were getting ready to leave he showed up with a
> big bag of money. Enough for Benny and Rose and me
> to live on for months. He kept poking this in my face,
> pretending to be concerned. He said, "Here, otherwise
> you'll all go hungry."*
>
> *I said, "David, you don't want to help me. You
> want to help my wife. And nobody pays for her but
> me."*
>
> *He said, "What's the difference?"*
>
> *I said, "The difference is you hate my guts and this
> is your way of pointing out that you're rich and I'm not.
> Stop being a jerk."*
>
> *We didn't need his money anyway. I went out and
> got our own funds together doing what I had to do. Basically, trading junk in the market. So three weeks after
> I got back we had enough to leave.*

Benny's brother Manny lives in a Displaced Person's camp in Austria, a country now controlled by the United States army. The letter he sent to Benny says the DP camp is a safe haven for Jews. After walking, hitchhiking, and hopping a train down through Czechoslovakia the trio arrive at the Danube. The long river divides the American and Russian zones. Blue alpine water sparkles under the bridge.

To cross over and begin their new lives the travelers must get past armed guards. They have no pass so William tries to sweet-talk the soldier in the guardhouse at the entrance to the bridge. The MP pulls a chunky black Colt .45 and orders all three refugees to get off the bridge and go back where they came from.

They regroup at an outdoor café where coffee is expensive and the waiter turns his nose up at their shabby clothes. But the table gives them a good view of the bridge and time to strategize. There is no way they can go back to the land of mass graves and bloody riots. And after six Nazi camps one gruff sentry is not the most intimidating obstacle in the world.

Two long streetcars cross the bridge every hour at exactly the same time, one from the Russian side, one from the American. For two minutes, moving in opposite directions, they completely block the guardhouse view of the left side of the bridge.

"In the camps you developed a sixth sense called sneakiness," William says. "I grabbed Rose and we used the streetcars as camouflage while we jogged across. This was in broad daylight and we had suitcases so it was a lot trickier than it sounds. Smuggling her over went perfect but it took me four tries and four hours before I could go back and get Benny across."

Thousands of survivors fill the spartan DP camp on the outskirts of Linz. The Schiffs will live here from 1946 until the summer of 1949. Quarters are cramped but there are schools, shops, religious services, and the physical safety Benny's brother promised.

William starts trading in his barrack. The refugees need someone to help them broker unwanted possessions for necessities. His customers soon include farmers in the surrounding countryside who need gasoline controlled by American soldiers. The GIs, in turn, need cigarettes and William ends up working as a courier for an American lieutenant who dabbles in business on both sides of the border. From a motorcycle William upgrades to a covered jeep and takes on another survivor as a partner. It is never easy.

"We were trapped in the DP camp for almost four years while the UN tried to figure out what to do. Rose had to stand in line all the time for rations and I didn't like living off charity. So I put a lot of miles on the bike and the jeep and made my own money."

No longer hunted animals, the couple can enjoy each other's human company. Rosalie quickly becomes pregnant.

"The Germans took everything from me," she says, "and I wanted something of my own, something little I could hold. Michael was one of the first children born after the war. How lucky I was to be able to conceive this child."

She has a big trust issue with the German doctors who staff the delivery room.

> *Back in Krakow when the Germans were liquidating the ghetto I saw a soldier run a bayonet through a very pregnant woman. He stuck the knife right through the hand she was using to shield her belly. Once I started to show, whenever we went outside to walk around*

in the streets I always covered my stomach with both hands.

I didn't exactly know how babies were born. When I watched the Russian girl in the bed next to me have her baby it scared me to death. My labor was tough because I had hernias from all the heavy lifting in the camps. It went on forever and I yelled the whole time while the Russian girl laughed. But Michael came out fine, ten and a half pounds.

During selections in the camps the first Jewish males killed were young boys and old men. One scholar described this targeting strategy as an attempt to destroy the soul of Judaism by breaking the link between grandfather and grandson, a key continuum of Jewish lineage. Rosalie is thankful the camps did not interrupt her family line.

"From the first day, it was incredible how much of my father I see in Michael. As he has grown up, he shows the same philanthropic inclination, the same concern for other people. I do not know where my father died, but through my children I am able to witness his heart still doing good in this world every day. So in spite of everything we went through, I can say with great pride today: '*dor l'dor*'. From generation to generation."

During the pregnancy, William had an accident.

In a snow storm one night my partner and I hit a patch of ice on a mountain road. We flipped down the embankment three times loaded with a dozen giant cans full of gas. Nothing exploded that time but a few weeks later I set myself on fire portioning gas from can to can.

*It was raining that day so I had to fill the gaso-
line cans in the little apartment we had just moved
into. The baby was on the floor and Rose was cooking.
There must have been a spark because suddenly I was
wrapped up in fire. I hauled the two big cans outside
so they wouldn't explode but slipped and fell down in a
puddle. I was drenched in gas.*

Rosalie remembers the rainy afternoon well:

*I was frying fish and didn't hear a thing. When I turned
to check on the baby I saw William through the door.
He was on fire outside flapping his arms like a movie
stuntman. I thought, my God, this is a man of endless
troubles.*

*When we put the fire out he was in shock. But he
drove the jeep to the hospital himself. His head and
clothes were smoking the whole way. His face, arms,
and hands were black with first-degree burns. The doctors said he might be disfigured for life but he healed
fine.*

The UN relief agency asks William to name three pre-
ferred destination countries. He chooses the United States,
Canada, and Australia. When the Schiffs are accepted into
the US the agency tells him that New York is overcrowded and
no longer an option.

*I didn't know any other places in America so I told
the secretary to decide. She said, "Great, we'll send you
to Texas. Nobody wants to go to Texas." We sailed in*

July from Bremenhaven for New Orleans on a troop
ship taking sailors home. The USS General LeRoy
Eltinge was the biggest thing Rose or I had ever seen.
To help cover passage I worked in the galley three weeks
and peeled a mountain of potatoes.

After three weeks the soldiers sighted land and
started shouting and slapping each other on the back.
There was a band playing when we docked and thou-
sands of family members and wives holding up babies
and crying. Michael was three by then. We each took
him by a hand and walked down this long gangplank
into all the music and cheering and a sea of flags. I will
never forget that day. See, I'm crying now. God bless
this country.

The Jewish Community Center buys train tickets to Dallas. Four days after the Schiffs move into their first apartment
Rosalie's heart sinks. Someone has marked a swastika on the
door.

"It was just some neighborhood kids who heard us speaking Polish and thought we were evil German Nazis. My first
reaction was, 'O my God, here we go again.' But all the neigh-
bors were very kind."

The few Hollywood westerns that made their way to Krakow led the couple to expect a Texas of tumbleweeds and
stockyards. Dallas turns out to be a clean, white-collar city that
has boomed during the war. Rosalie's real new enemy looms
overhead from June through August.

The heat was something else. We came before air con-
ditioning so I had to lie in the bathtub a lot. At dinner

*the three of us would sit at the table sweating like crazy.
After two years Michael asked me, "Mom, why do we
always eat soup in the summer?"*

*I thought it was a strange question. Soup is what
people ate in Poland all the time. He said that when
he went to his friends' houses they ate salads and sand-
wiches and cold cuts. It was quite a revelation. Today,
I can cook all kinds of American food. I even make
enchiladas.*

William's first job is as a janitor at a company that sells sewing machines. "I was thirty years old, making sixty-five cents
an hour sweeping and cleaning like I did when I was thirteen.
We had very little furniture and Rose and I sold fish on the
side for extra money. We went up to a lake north of Dallas
and bought these big buffalo carp to sell to other Jews."

City Sewing Machines has a repair shop. When one of
the mechanics retires, William takes his job. After his English
improves he gets into sales. Three years later he averages $200
a week in commissions.

"One day I went to the office downtown to file some paperwork," he recalls. "The street was lined with people and I
stood there while the big convertible went by with President
Kennedy and his wife. They waved at us. We waved at them. I
walked into the office and the secretary yelled, 'They shot the
President!' I told her that couldn't be true because I just saw
him two minutes ago."

A daughter Rachel is born and, two years later, a son Bobby. The Schiffs buy a house and a car and earn their citizen-
ship. Rosalie works as a beautician until William opens his
own business where she does the books. Investing their sav-

ings in an apartment building, they begin a successful career in commercial real estate. Today the couple have four grand-children and two step-grandchildren. Rachel, Bobby, and Michael have all traveled back to Krakow with their parents to try to understand the history that still torments them. Rosalie is frank about her struggles with the past.

> We are damaged people, no doubt about it. You don't come through something like the Holocaust smelling like a flower. For forty years I hid my past in my heart. I was afraid of vacuum cleaners, mailmen, police officers, anybody in a uniform. I was terrified to let my children out of my sight. The toast would pop up in the toaster and I would jump through the ceiling with it.
>
> For forty years I never wanted anybody to ask me what religion I am and I never told anybody my religion. It took me some time to make peace with God, but I did that. He doesn't teach us bad things.
>
> Years ago in downtown Dallas I saw a dress in the window of Neiman Marcus, a spring print with bright flowers. Part of my heart wanted it, part said I could never wear such joyful colors. I turned to walk away and saw my reflection in the store window. I saw myself in the filthy green skirt I wore for years in the camps, the skirt painted with yellow stripes to mark me as a Jew. It was a pretty day and all these happy Texans were walking past me but I was still back in Poland with my cart full of bodies.
>
> I went home to my nice living room and started asking myself questions. Am I alive? Did I go really through those things? Who are you, Rosalie?

> One of the ladies whose hair I did was a psycholo-
> gist. We got to know each other and she gave me a few
> books that I found fascinating. I went to college, studied
> psychology, and after some counseling, little by little, I
> started to get better.
>
> I finally went out and bought my own happy dress
> and asked William to take me dancing. We went to
> a nice hotel downtown and saw a band called the Joe
> Reichman Orchestra. We started doing this regularly. It
> must have brightened me up because one night I won a
> bottle of champagne in a cha-cha contest.

During a recent trip to Argentina the couple visited Oskar Schindler's wife Emelie. Still lucid in her nineties and supported by the Jewish community, she lived with her cats in a small flat on the outskirts of Buenos Aires.

"I thanked her for what her husband did for me," Rosalie says, "and we talked about Amon Goeth. She said that the spooky thing about such haters is how well they wear their masks, how charming and normal they can seem. She was a very good person and she said she wished her marriage could have worked but Oskar was a hard drinker and a womanizer."

Another trip was less pleasant.

> We went back to Krakow with Michael, our daughter
> Rachel, and two of our grandchildren not too long ago.
> At three o'clock in the morning I woke up screaming.
> I don't know if it was a dream or an anxiety attack or
> what it was. I kept yelling, "Don't you see them killing
> on the streets? Look how much blood there is!" William
> had to slap me to bring me back to my senses.

We went to the apartment on Dietlovska Street and said a prayer for my family. The same Polish woman who was so cruel half a century earlier was still living there. I couldn't believe it. She was very old and almost deaf. I asked her if I could show the apartment to us and offered her ten dollars for her trouble. She didn't slam the door in my face this time.

Later that day we bought bread at a bakery. Walking in the streets of Kazimierz something came over me. I started to eat the bread like I was starving again. I held the loaf close to my body with both hands and I didn't want to share it, not even with my husband and son. I couldn't help myself. I would not let go of that loaf of bread.

A few memories I still suppress. You can't remember what you have to forget. William wakes up screaming at night. Sometimes he's buried alive again, sometimes it's his mother begging him to save her. We each handle it in our own way. He talks and I cry. Half a century and the heart is still broken.

On our fortieth anniversary I finally had a proper wedding. In the video I'm all smiles until the rabbi mentions the Holocaust. Suddenly my face goes blank. I was fifty-nine and still didn't want to talk about it. On our sixtieth anniversary we got married a third time. By then I had told my story to 15,000 school children.

Speaking of marriage ceremonies I was pleased to learn that Mania survived. Like us, she was saved by the United States. William and I went to her daughter's wedding and this sweet girl looked very beautiful in her gown. That day I consider a triumph.

chapter twelve

The future of hate

Warsaw ghetto fighter Alexander Donat did not consider the Holocaust the last chapter in the book of human cruelty. He saw it as the preface to a future age of total chaos. With great passion and urgency Donat warned that a new generation would destroy the world with nuclear war unless mankind could keep hate from seizing power again.

Near the site of the Kennedy assassination, the West End district in downtown Dallas is a collection of old warehouses that have been redone as restaurants, shops, and nightclubs. The temporary quarters of the Dallas Holocaust Museum occupy a corner by an old railroad track. William and Rosalie lecture here at least twice a week.

In the auditorium today they tell the short version of their story to eighty-three seventh graders from a suburban school district. It's a tale that museum director Elliott Dlin is careful to put in context.

"The Schiffs are very much the exception," he says.

> *They survived the Holocaust; most did not. So we shouldn't look for patterns or models of survival. The*

truth is that many other victims probably did exactly what they did and were killed, while others survived by making very different choices. Their stories show that one never knew and never could know what to do or what was coming next. In Goeth's camp, William stood third in line and survived. At Belzec his brother Bronek snuck into the wrong line and was murdered. Searching for patterns or explanations in the testimony of survivors is like trying to put together a jigsaw puzzle with six million missing pieces.

It's hard for Rosalie to re-tell her story and re-live her pain over and over again. Each time she speaks at the Museum her blood pressure goes up and she has trouble sleeping that night. But she has a mission and her testimony makes a big impression.

Uniformly quiet and attentive, the kids today scrunch up their noses at the gruesome parts of the narrative. Questions from young Americans in the twenty-first century are revealing. One girl asks Rosalie what she missed most in the camps: dresses or makeup.

"Food," laughs the eighty-four-year-old.

The kids nod. They are ten minutes away from a field trip lunch at the Old Spaghetti Warehouse. When a small shy boy asks William why the numbers on his left arm haven't rubbed off after all these years, a stout classmate scoffs loudly enough for all to hear: "It's a *tattoo*, stupid."

Rosalie uses her microphone to explain and correct.

"They pushed the ink all the way down into his skin, honey, so it's going to last as long as he does. And let's not be making fun of one another, okay? That's how the Holocaust got started. Harsh words lead to hard actions. That's the message here today, kids."

The tattooed man intrigues the children. William addressed them earlier in front of a display that includes the uniform he wore at Buchenwald. "You weighed *sixty-nine* pounds?" a pixie girl gasps. "*I* weigh more than that."

Onward to their pasta, the rosy-cheeked students file out into the heat past a large photo of pale Jewish corpses. Balancing against her walker, Rosalie steps off the curb in front of the museum and settles gingerly onto her scalding car seat. It is 102 degrees outside. "Pretty please, sun, go away," she huffs. As the car climbs up on a highway she has a chance to critique her performance.

"That was a lot less nerve-wracking than the teleconference yesterday. Yesterday it was three schools and 300 students on three different TV screens. The kids were shooting questions so fast I could never figure out who was talking."

An hour later the Schiffs relax at their kitchen table. At eighty-eight, William has diabetes and must perform his blood sugar ritual. "Yesterday I went to a new doctor," he says, pricking his finger and daubing the blood drop on the test paper. "He said, 'You look great, Mr. Schiff. I can see you've had a very easy life.' I said, 'You're right, doctor, every day just like a fairy tale.'"

A small TV in the corner shows images from Baghdad, more corpses attributed to the "Black Crow" death squads working out of the Iraqi Interior Ministry. William sighs.

*I know hatred so well. It used to boil inside me because
of the helplessness and frustration I felt in those days.
I was the oldest male in my family and I thought I*

was a big shot. All the little cousins like Zofi looked up to me and I couldn't do a thing to help them. I had to watch them die. The Germans killed my parents in their early forties. My brother was eighteen, my sister in her twenties. Because I refused to leave Krakow nobody survived. I've lived with it sixty-six years.

At Auschwitz I thought the Germans had also killed my gorgeous nineteen-year-old wife. I swore I'd stay alive so I could start killing Germans the second I got free. And what happened? I didn't have it in me. Why didn't I help the Russian prisoners throw the German women off the bridge? There was the revenge I'd been dreaming of night after night.

What happened was I forgot they were German. I just saw two women in trouble. Two human beings getting victimized because they were members of a hated nationality. Was the mother married to an SS guy? So what? Was that her fault? What right did I have to punish her? Or to punish her daughter, a teenager with no involvement in politics? What would I gain from it?

Today I'm glad I never hurt anybody. You kill yourself when you hate. It's the worst disease in the world and it took me forever to get all the way through it. That's why we always tell the kids there's only one race: the human race.

Rosalie takes a call from a junior college professor. Next week she will tell her story to 400 students, her twelfth year to speak at this campus.

Some people think mass hatred can't be checked with education. I strongly disagree. We've told our story to more than 20,000 students now and I know from the letters they send me that it makes a big difference.

Last week I spoke at a mosque, the first time I've ever been inside one. Such a lovely place, all white inside with white ruffles on the chairs. I was leaning on my walker surrounded by big Arab men and it made me a little nervous.

Why? Because of stereotypes. And it was obvious at first that maybe they would rather not hear some stranger tell a long sad story. Maybe some of them believe the new President of Iran when he says the Holocaust never happened.

But you know what? These gracious Muslim men listened politely for more than an hour. I got a standing ovation and I opened up some minds. Absolutely. I can tell by looking at the faces when I'm done. And a lot more people at home got the message because Channel 11 was there with cameras.

So don't listen to people who tell you nothing can be done. Look at the progress that's been made in race relations here in the United States. When we first came to Texas in 1948 I was shocked at the way black people were oppressed. I was afraid I would be treated the same way. When you've been a slave you understand.

"We weren't slaves, Rose. The Germans just pushed us around."

"We were slaves, William."

"If you think so, okay. I don't see it that way. What's important is we didn't waste our time today if only one kid got the message. Because the one kid who gives in to hate will do more bad in his lifetime than a hundred good kids will do good. The danger is always there. People are still using politics and religion to make trouble."

Sixty years after the Holocaust, neuroscientists are using thermal imaging to search the brain for the roots of hate. In a world full of ethnic and spiritual rivalries, the enigmatic emotion is more dangerous than ever when shared by a group. What enables societies to justify ethnic purges and genocide? What specific circumstances spark the brutality and massacres? How can moral authorities in a destructive culture keep the innocent from becoming victims?

A new site has been acquired in Dallas for a permanent Holocaust Museum and an innovative Center for Education and Tolerance. The mission of the unique teaching facility is to reduce prejudice and promote tolerance among future generations. Michael Schiff sees the center as a community-wide effort of national significance, squarely in the American tradition.

Like most immigrants, my family has a deep love for this country's classic values. Things like acceptance, tolerance, equality, and respect. We appreciate our freedoms and believe the best way to protect democracy is to practice it. My parents know what can happen when people forget their humanity and give way to indifference, so they try to do what they can to make sure that doesn't happen again. Their concern is not unreasonable in a world where Holocaust deniers from thirty dif-

ferent countries recently gathered in Tehran to challenge and refute the accepted version of events. It's hard to believe, but radical hatred armed with modern military technology has the potential to make the horrors of the past look like nothing

Rosalie anticipates with great joy the day the facility will open to the public and the labor of love can continue on a scale demanded in a new age of terror.

Who will teach the next generation that social justice is their responsibility? Who will teach them it's their duty to protect all human beings from persecution and violence? One crazy insecure man tried to destroy my people. He almost got away with it, thanks to millions of supporters who blamed other people for their own failures and unhappiness. Such madmen can only come to power in a vacuum and the new center in Dallas will help prevent such a vacuum.

In my dreams for years now I have seen a door. In these dreams, always the same, Nazis are chasing me and trying to take my grandchildren away from me. I always try to lead the children through this very special door. For some reason I feel they will find safety on the other side. Who knows? Maybe it's the door to the new center. I hope I live long enough to see it.

KEY TO INTER-CHAPTER PHOTOS

The views or opinions expressed in this book, and the context in which the images are used, do not necessarily reflect the views or policy of, nor imply approval or endorsement by, the United States Holocaust Memorial Museum (USHMM).

Photo after Chapter:
1. *Hans Frank entertains Heinrich Himmler at Wawel Castle, 1940*
   USHMM photo archive
2. *Deportation during Krakow ghetto liquidation, March, 1943*
   USHMM photo archive
3. *Amon Goeth on the balcony of his villa at Plaszow*
   USHMM photo archive
4. *A women's camp*
   USHMM photo archive
5. *Transport trains at Auschwitz-Birkenau arrival ramp*
   USHMM photo archive
6. *A public hanging*
   USHMM photo archive
7. *"Hero" portrait of Hitler*
   USHMM photo archive
8. *Rescued camp survivors in hospital barracks*
   USHMM photo archive
9. *Liberated survivor at Buchenwald*
   US National Archives photo
10. *Street scene in Kazimierz*
    USHMM photo archive
11. *USS General LeRoy Eltinge*
    US National Archives photo

FOR FURTHER READING

For an overview of the broader political context, Richard J. Evans has been deservedly praised for *The Coming of the Third Reich* and *The Third Reich in Power* (The Penguin Press, 2003 and 2005). *The Jews of Krakow* by Eugeniusz Duda (Wydanictwo, Hagada and Argona-Jarden Jewish Bookshop) is an outstanding cultural history and provided especially helpful information on the city and the neighborhood of Kazimierz.

Professor Neil Kressel raises interesting questions about the psychological dynamics of genocide in *Mass Hate* (Westview Press, 2002.) The strategies and campaigns of the first Nazi killing teams are explained with great authority by Richard Rhodes in *Masters of Death: The SS-Einsatzgruppen and the Invention of the Holocaust* (Alfred A. Knopf, 2002).

Himmler, by Peter Padfield (Henry Holt and Co., 1990) is a telling portrait of power and bureaucracy run amok, and the memoir *Let Me Go, by* Helga Schneider (Walker & Co, 2004) offers an eerie modern encounter with an unrepentant SS loyalist.